MAINE
BOOK OF THE
DEAD

Memento Mori

MAINE
BOOK
OF THE
DEAD

GRAVEYARD LEGENDS
AND LORE

Roxie J. Zwicker

Roxie J. Zwicker

THE
History
PRESS

Published by The History Press
Charleston, SC
www.historypress.com

Cover image: The gravestone of Robert Cutt Whipple, dated to 1761, at the Kittery Point, Maine cemetery.

All images are courtesy of author unless otherwise stated.

First published 2021

Manufactured in the United States

ISBN 9781467150316

Library of Congress Control Number: 2021938398

Notice: The information in this book is true and complete to the best of our knowledge. It is offered without guarantee on the part of the author or The History Press. The author and The History Press disclaim all liability in connection with the use of this book.

CONTENTS

INTRODUCTION

There are a few essential elements you find in the spirit of a Mainer. A humble appreciation of well-crafted things, wit dry enough you may not know when the joke ends and when it begins and, most importantly, a love for the land and the sea.
—Anthony Bourdain

It was a road trip like so many others. Packed in the trunk of our car was our cooler for the day, filled with cold drinks and favorite snacks to keep us going on this next adventure. I've been taking road trips throughout New England for as long as I can remember, but this one was going to be a little bit different. There is something about exploring the wilds of the Maine north woods and trusting the meandering line in our companion map book to guide us—first on pavement, then on dirt and finally along rugged rocks. That rocky terrain was more suitable for a 4x4 vehicle than for the small sedan that I had been driving, and I was thankful that before this trip I had put four brand-new tires on the car. The map did not indicate that this was a logging road, but it soon became very apparent that there was no one else traveling this road other than the massive logging trucks that could be seen along the connecting paths. The thicket of trees that surrounded us was accompanied by the occasional dirt cloud that usually made it difficult to see and navigate the road ahead. Although the day was beautiful and the sky was crystal blue up above, these were roads unlike any I had traveled before.

I was thankful to see a yellow slash painted on a stone or a tree alongside the road every once in a while, reminding me that I was still on the correct path even though I was feeling doubtful. My cellular devices were more than doubtful—they were struggling, with no service for hours. The woods seemed vast and unending, infinite by all accounts; it was almost spectacular except for the fact that I didn't know exactly where I was. The blue color of the car I was driving turned brown with the road dust, but with my hands planted firmly at ten and two on the steering wheel, I continued on. At a bend in the road, I saw it: Mount Katahdin, looming at 5,269 feet. It is part of the Appalachian chain of mountains and the highest peak in Maine.

"What a place to live, die and be buried in!" wrote Henry David Thoreau after his Katahdin ascent in 1846. "There, certainly, men would live forever, and laugh at death and the grave." There have been many deaths on Katahdin over its recorded history, from people struck down by lightning strikes to injuries that incapacitated people trying to find their way off the mountain. Some people who have died on the mountain have been returned there from the scattering of ashes by loved ones.

As the mountain remained in my view beyond patches of bogs, swamps and clusters of gnarled pine trees, I thought about how the mountain was a hallowed ground all its own for those who escaped to find nature but never returned. Katahdin rose up out of the ground and connected the earth to the sky in a dramatic manner, and somewhere in my mind I could also see it as a spiritual marker, not unlike so many gravestones whose carvings I've stopped to read. I continued driving, and the mountain slipped away from my view as large signs for paper companies that were logging the road came into view. The large logging trucks became more frequent as I pulled to the side of the road and watched the freshly cut timbers go past in blinding dust clouds.

As I started to make my way toward the end of the road, I opened the windows of my car and breathed deep the smells of fresh-cut wood and the rich earthiness of the greenery. The trees of the rugged north woods of Maine have been harvested for countless generations and form a stunning natural resource in both size and scale. My mind raced back in time to the loggers with hand tools and the men who worked along the rivers to drive those logs from sunup to sundown. If there was an accident and someone died at a lumber camp or drowned in the river, they were often buried in the woods without a gravestone. I wondered if there was anyone buried near where I had stopped along the side of the road.

One thing is for certain about Maine: the heritage of a hardy and hardworking people was going to be found in more than just the burial grounds. Their stories are in the woods; on the mountaintops; along lonely,

The logging roads of Maine lead to the breathtaking wilderness of this rugged state.

weather-beaten islands; and spread out over thousands of miles both settled and wild. In writing this book, I am looking to share the stories reflecting the spirit of Maine found in its graveyards and sleeping in its ancient places. Come and take a journey with me, and I promise you will find Maine and its people inspiring and unforgettable.

DISCOVERING HISTORIC MAINE GRAVEYARDS

On March 15, 1820, Maine took its place as the twenty-third state in the United States. Originally the province of Maine, governed by the State of Massachusetts, Maine established the motto of *Dirigo*, which is Latin for "I lead," upon attaining statehood. The seal of the state features many of the symbols that people associate with Maine, such as a moose, a farmer and a sailor. Today, the state is made up of 430 towns, 22 cities, 46 plantations and 41 unorganized townships, as well as countless graveyards to match. Nearly 90 percent of Maine is forested, with a rugged beauty; within the shadows of those woods are captivating stories of those who lived their lives through hard work in a wilderness land that reaches into the sea.

Visiting the cemeteries in Maine is one way to explore all the region has to offer, including its remote places and natural beauty. There are also places to go wandering and discover memorials to those whose spirit is still alive in the hearts of many. You can walk down beach pathways and find memorial benches and stones reminding us of those who loved Maine and those who called it home. Small burial grounds can be found next to the old fortifications in Maine, providing history lessons about how the area was shaped and those who were shaped by it.

Some folks in Maine say that you can't call yourself a Mainer unless you were born in Maine; however, that hasn't stopped thousands of people from spending time in this beckoning "Vacationland." The gravestones that stand in Maine's cemeteries tell us how people fought, worshiped and played,

Left: The open gate of Pond Grove Cemetery on Peaks Island invites visitors in to view the gravestones that date back to the nineteenth century.

Right: The granite Fisherman's Memorial in St. George stands at the center of a compass rose and honors eleven local men who have died at sea since 1941.

such as veterans' memorial plaques, religious iconography and carvings of lobster boats, to name a few. Each cemetery is the reflective timeline of a community and is one of the best places to explore to get a sense of the history of a city or town.

Maine has a great abundance of folklore. Storytelling here is so important, whether told around a crackling campfire or passed down in grandma's kitchen while making blueberry pie. You will discover tales of superstition in some burial grounds or read a verse of good old "Downeast" wisdom carved on some gravestones. This book invites you to take a look at discovering Maine through its historic graveyards and awaken the memory of the lives of those who are buried there.

AN EARLY LANDSCAPE OF DEATH

The First Known Burying Grounds

Some experts believe that the area we now know as Maine has been inhabited since 3000 BC. Scholars and archaeologists theorize that there were Vikings who visited the area between northern Maine and Newfoundland. There is even a suggestion that they may have built short-term settlements there in their travels. There are mysterious carved figures that have been discovered on the basaltic rocks on the shores of Machias. In 1979, researchers positively identified a piece of coin found at Blue Hill as a genuine Norse or Viking coin. The coin was estimated to be more than nine hundred years old and is believed to be the oldest known European artifact found in North America.

There are published reports about the Red Paint People, who were early inhabitants of the area. The reason for their name is because they lined the graves of their dead with red clay, with some of that clay believed to have been dug out from the side of Mount Katahdin. Experts claim that these people hunted swordfish and did some trading but mostly kept to themselves. Some of these older burial sites have revealed the presence of red ochre and crushed hematite. No one is quite certain what happened to the Red Paint People. Many studies and years of research have led to no definite answers. They may have moved on, assimilated into other groups or developed illnesses. Perhaps we will know one day.

Countless records of ancient bones being discovered all over the state have been recorded along with precious artifacts, such as handcrafted tools, jewelry and ritual items. Shell middens have been discovered along Maine's

Over the years, people have found gravestones as old as 1652 at the Old Burying Ground in Pemaquid.

coast, indicating where native villages once stood and where burial remains might exist. During the nineteenth century, many findings from excavations of native remains were sent to Harvard University in Boston for further research. Great care is taken by modern-day researchers to leave the known locations undisturbed. However, due to construction and road and highway expansions, these sites are still being unearthed.

I remember speaking to a woman in Kittery who told me that she couldn't understand why there were strange-shaped mounds on her property. She described feeling "energy" from them and decided to have an expert on Native American graves come and investigate. He explained to her that it was a native burial ground from the way it was situated on the property. She then told me that she felt proud to be the keeper of the land the burial ground was on and that she would make sure it was not disturbed.

There are countless cemeteries that have been moved over the years in Maine as well, so it can be hard to put a date on them, if they can be found at all. Take, for example, the cemeteries in the villages of Flagstaff, Dead River and Bigelow, Maine. In 1950, Central Maine Power flooded the three

Quality slate has been quarried in Monson for more than 150 years; while some unused sections of the quarry are flooded, slate excavations still continue in the area today.

towns to create a storage reservoir. The twenty-seven-mile lake that was created required flooding twenty thousand acres to generate power in the summer to a hydroelectric dam in Bigelow. All three cemeteries were dug up and were moved to a cemetery on Route 27 in Eustis, Maine. So it can be hard to locate some original cemeteries and date them.

The oldest common burying ground (a burying place used by the community at large) for seventeenth-century settlers in Maine is the Eastern Cemetery in Portland. Most early graveyards were small plots used by families. In 1895, *Maine Historical Magazine* wrote of the early graves in Maine:

> *The vast majority of the dead have no gravestones. The dead were buried deep in the earth, with their feet towards the east and the graves almost filled with cobblestones for protection against wild animals. Field stones marked the early graves, one at the head and another at the foot. Few gravestones were set up prior to 1670; then slate gravestones from the west of England came very small and very thick, and upon them rude hands traced the initials of the dead. Between 1690 and 1710 larger slate stones came with elaborate skulls and cherub faces. Many of these stones are broken and have wasted away, while some are so well preserved that today the faint lines made by the engraver to guard him in the height of letters, are still as distinct as they were 150 or 200 years ago. Between 1700 and the breaking out of the Revolutionary war, the slate of the West of England, of different colors and qualities was almost universally used.*

As time went on, the abundant resources of Maine contributed to its cemeteries. The Monson slate quarry was a resource for the much-needed slate for gravestones. In fact, the slate excavated from the quarry was so desirable that the grave markers for President John F. Kennedy and his wife, Jacqueline Kennedy Onassis, were made from Monson slate.

Generations of gravestone-carving families could also be found throughout the state of Maine. Many of the oldest gravestones in the state can be found in the southern region of Maine, so that is where our journey will begin.

SOUTHERN MAINE
AND THE BEACHES

LIZZIE BOURNE, HOPE CEMETERY, KENNEBUNK MAINE

The rugged, frosty slopes of Mount Washington, New Hampshire, seem far away from the coastal community of Kennebunk, Maine, yet the two locations will forever be connected by the story of twenty-two-year-old Lizzie Bourne. It was September 14, 1855, and the trees along the ridges of Mount Washington were turning vibrant colors of orange and red, spearing through the morning mists. It seemed as though it would be a good day for a hike—just delayed until conditions cleared a bit for the four-mile hike up Mount Washington. Lizzie's uncle George and cousin Lucy decided that they were going to make the journey together with her, as the remainder of their vacationing group chose to remain at the mountain base hotel.

After an uneventful three-hour climb, the group had made it to a point near the carriage road about three miles from the mountain summit. As this was the nineteenth century, the clothing worn by the young women was not conducive for hiking, with all of the additional material and weight. Shoes were not protective on the uneven and changeable surfaces of the mountain. It became more and more difficult for the group to ascend the mountain, and as the sky grew dark, Lizzie became exhausted. The pressure of the escalating winds also proved challenging for the group, making it difficult to even stand.

LIZZIE G. BOURNE
AGED 23 YEARS
DAUGHTER OF EDW. E. BOURNE
OF KENNEBUNK, MAINE

HERE IN THE TWILIGHT COLD
AND GRAY,
LIFELESS, BUT BEAUTIFUL
SHE LAY,
AND FROM THE SKY SERENE
AND FAR,
A VOICE FELL LIKE A FALLING
STAR,
EXCELSIOR

THIS MONUMENT WAS MEANT FOR
THE TOP OF MOUNT WASHINGTON, BUT
ITS ERECTION THERE WAS PREVENTED
BY THE FAILURE OF THE PROJECTED ROAD.

The monument crafted in memory of the death of Lizzie Bourne was originally meant to be erected on Mount Washington.

In desperation, Lizzie's uncle tried to build a makeshift stone wall to protect his daughter and niece, as the decision was made to spend the night on the mountain. He tried to huddle together with the young women to keep them warm from the increasingly biting wind and rapidly dropping temperatures. Despite all of his efforts, around 10:00 p.m. that night, Lizzie stopped breathing. As night turned into day, the two survivors of the party made it to the Summit House on top of Mount Washington, which they did not realize was quite close to where they had spent the night.

Joseph Seavey Hall, who built the house on top of the mountain, was heading up toward the summit when someone told him about the tragedy the night before. He went to the Halfway House on the mountain to have a wooden coffin assembled to carry the body of the young woman. Down a narrow path from the mountain, a group of men carried the coffin with a silent Lizzie, alongside the melancholy family members. When Lizzie's father, Edward Bourne, found out what happened, he was completely heartbroken, having already buried his wife three years prior to Lizzie's death.

Joseph Hall sent a letter to Lizzie's father explaining that he marked the location of her death on the mountain, "placed with my own hands, the pile of stone, with a rose-quartz cap, on the spot that marks the place where she died." Lizzie's father commissioned a large memorial marker to be placed on the exact location where she died on Mount Washington; however, the stone is found at the Hope Cemetery in Kennebunk, and it tells the story:

> *This monument was meant for the top of Mt. Washington but its erection there was prevented by the failure of the projected road. In the afternoon of September 14, 1855 Miss Bourne with her uncle and cousin attempted to climb this mountain, but her strength suddenly failed from the wet, cold blast. They sought the poor shelter of these rocks and here about 10 at night she expired in consequence. It is thought of a heart disease fatally aggravated by toil and fatigue.*
>
> *Mount, sinless spirit, to thy destined rest!*
> *Whilst I (reversed our nature's kindlier doom) pour forth a father's sorrows o'er thy tomb.*
>
> *Lizzie G. Bourne*
> *Aged 23 Years*
> *Daughter of Edw. E. Bourne*
> *of Kennebunk, Maine.*
>
> *She had a lively intellect, a joyous heart,*
> *and strong affections, and was to her kindred*
> *and friends inexpressibly dear.*
>
> *Here in the twilight cold and gray,*
> *Lifeless, but beautiful, she lay,*
> *And far from the sky serene and far,*
> *A voice fell like a falling star.*
> *Excelsior!*

After Lizzie was laid to rest, her loss was felt far and wide by those who knew her and the community at large. There were several portraits of her painted after her death, one of which can be found at the nearby Brick Store Museum. Lizzie's friends were curious about whether they could speak to her in the afterlife and conducted a séance to explore lingering questions. Just over a year after her death, Lizzie's uncle George passed away at the age of fifty-five on December 7, 1856. Some believe that his guilt over the death of Lizzie contributed to his weakened condition, and he died from typhoid fever. He is also buried at the Hope Cemetery in Kennebunk, not too far away from Lizzie.

A wooden marker stands today on Mount Washington and reads the same as the inscription found on the gravestone in Kennebunk. For years, the tradition has been to leave a stone in memory of Lizzie on the fateful spot on Mount Washington, and a pyramid of stones has formed at the bottom of the memorial to Lizzie. There are some trail guides and visitors who say that the mountain is haunted by the spirit of Lizzie. A young girl in a white, flowing Victorian dress can be seen on the trails to remind people about how dangerous it can be.

OLD FIELDS BURIAL GROUND, SOUTH BERWICK

When the Old Fields Burial Ground was established in the seventeenth century for the early settlement of Kittery Commons, most first graves were unmarked with traditional gravestones. In 1713, the settlement was incorporated as Berwick, and one hundred years later, South Berwick received its own designation and incorporation as a town. Located on the corner of Vine Street, this woodland cemetery seemed enchanted by the light of the day. As the sun shifts throughout the day, gravestones darken one by one and shift into shadows under the canopy of trees. During the height of summer, wildflowers fill the small walking paths between the stones.

A blanket of pine needles covers the grave of Colonel Johnathan Hamilton Jr., who died on September 26, 1802, at the age of fifty-seven. He was a successful shipbuilder and trade merchant, primarily sailing his vessels between Portsmouth, New Hampshire, and the West Indies. His magnificent Georgian mansion, built in 1785, overlooks the nearby Salmon Falls River and can be toured through Historic New England.

In this burial ground is the grave for Mehitable Goodwin, the wife of Thomas Goodwin. Her family was torn apart during the 1690 raid on nearby Salmon Falls. During this attack, the houses were burned, and many settlers were killed by an alliance of French troops and Wabanaki warriors.

The Old Fields Burial Ground in South Berwick is a beautiful woodland cemetery, but at one time the entire area was cleared of trees.

Mehitable, her husband and their five-month-old son were taken captive along with two dozen people from the community.

Husband and wife were separated on the long winter walk to Canada. Mehitable struggled to keep her baby nourished during the arduous ordeal. Puritan minister Cotton Mather wrote of the incident in 1702, explaining it in a dramatic and graphic manner: "He [a kidnapper] violently snatched the babe out of its mother's arms and before her face, knocked out its brains, and stripped it of the few rags it had hitherto enjoyed, and ordered her the task to go wash the bloody clothes."

The child's body was hung from a tree, and Mehitable was forced to continue on with the march north. She was sold into servitude in Quebec, and she eventually took on another name. In 1695, she was ransomed and returned to South Berwick. Her husband, Thomas, had escaped from Canada a few years before, and amazingly, they reunited and went on to have five more children. Mehitable died at the age of seventy in 1740; a footstone is all that remains to mark her burial site on the grounds.

The gravestone for Reverend John Tompson reads that he died on December 21, 1828, at the age of eighty-nine in the sixty-first year of his ministry. In 1791, as the minister of the First Parish Church, he climbed on a white horse and rode it all the way to Boston, Massachusetts, to obtain the school charter for Berwick Academy, signed by John Hancock.

A willow and urn are carved on the broken gravestone for Captain Elisha Hill, who was a local mill owner who died at the age of fifty-five on June 1, 1764. The inscription reads: "He left fourteen children who all followed him to the silent grave." The gravestone for Rhoda Lambert tells the story of her infant son, Thomas, who is buried at her side "aged 24 hours." The house the Lambert family lived in still stands today and is rumored to be haunted by the sounds of a baby crying in the middle of the night.

The Old Berwick Historical Society has been putting forth efforts over recent years to tell the stories of the people buried at Old Fields through tours and lectures. Volunteer groups have come together to keep the grounds well maintained and marked.

WENTWORTH TOMB

In New England, oftentimes when streets are named for families, their relics and remains are often nearby. Such is the case with the Wentworth Tomb in Kittery, Maine. The small graveyard and tomb are easily missed, as they sit next to a parking lot for a pizza parlor and dry cleaning business. In the 1960s, a TV and appliance store occupied the building next to the cemetery. As originally laid out, it would have been part of the property for the Wentworth house, which still stands nearby at no. 9 Wentworth Street.

General Wentworth was a physician from Kittery and served in the local militia. At the beginning of the Civil War, he worked as a storekeeper at the Portsmouth Naval Shipyard. In 1862, he raised the Twenty-Seventh Maine Infantry to defend Washington, D.C. He was injured in a mine explosion at the Siege of Petersburg, Virginia, in 1864. He resigned his commission shortly afterward and received a promotion to brigadier general for his service at the end of the war. Upon his return to Kittery, he served in many political capacities, including as Congressional representative for the First District of Maine. He died at the age of seventy-seven on July 12, 1897, and is entombed with his wife, Eliza Jane, who died in 1883, and their daughter, Annie, who died just short of sixteen years old in 1862. His portrait can be found on display at the Kittery Historical and Naval Museum.

The Wentworth tomb sits at the edge of an active business parking lot in Kittery.

There are a handful of other gravestones in front of the tomb, although it is believed that many original stones have been lost over the years due to development. In the summer, a dense perennial garden is tended to in the graveyard, a reminder of the past hiding in plain sight of modern structures.

PORTSMOUTH NAVAL SHIPYARD

The Portsmouth Naval Shipyard is located on what used to be more commonly known as Fernald's Island in Kittery, Maine. Since its early days, there has been a form of shipbuilding in the area, and in the 1790s, Secretary of the Navy Benjamin Stoddert commissioned the first federal shipyard. It took four years to build and establish the navy yard, which opened in 1800, making it the oldest operational naval yard in the United States today. While the early years were focused on shipbuilding, in 1898 Spanish prisoners were kept captive in a prison camp at the far end of the island. The Portsmouth Naval Prison, referred to by many as the "Alcatraz of the East," was built in 1905. The focus of the shipyard shifted to submarine building and overhauling, and today the work involves modernizing submarines. The official name, the Portsmouth Naval Shipyard, surprises many people, as the facility is located in Kittery, Maine, but boundary disputes were settled years ago to establish the definitive location.

There are a few burial grounds at the shipyard, including the Fernald family cemetery, which predates the military facility, and the U.S. Naval Shipyard cemetery. The shipyard cemetery was established in 1820 and completed in 1901. The first burial took place in December 1820, when Elisha Smith, a local civilian of Fernald's Island, was laid to rest. Among the three hundred graves are British pilots who lost their lives in World War II, as well as ten Danish and five British seamen who drowned when the British freighter HMS *Empire Knight* sank off the coast of Maine on February 11, 1944.

Located behind the museum is a fascinating animal cemetery for animals that had a service affiliation. The sign on the grounds reads: "Four animals are interred in the animal cemetery. They include 'Tom' a valiant horse ridden by Colonel Huntington, USMC, in Cuba during the 1898 war with Spain, and two bulldogs, 'Spike' and 'Chesty' who served with great zeal and fidelity as Marine Corps mascots while at the Shipyard. Also, here is 'Gyp' a mascot of the Naval Prison's Marine Detachment."

The Marine Corps mascot "Chesty" was named after U.S. Marine Corps lieutenant general Lewis Burwell "Chesty" Puller (June 26, 1898–October 11, 1971). General Puller was one of the most decorated members of the Marine Corps. He is the only marine and one of two U.S. servicemen to ever be awarded five Navy Crosses. The grave marker for Chesty reads:

> *Semper Fidelis, Derby's Chauncey of Bullmede, "Chesty" 13 August 1964 to 16 September 1965. A faithful friend.*

A few steps away from Chesty is a gravestone that has a bulldog in a spiked collar engraved on it, and it reads:

> *Cpl. HJ Spike, USMC Bulldog Mascot, 11 Feb 1982–27 Jan 1986, Served with dignity and honor. A true "Devil Dog" and friend.*

The only horse to be buried in the Portsmouth Naval Shipyard animal cemetery is Old Tom. He served with the U.S. marines in Cuba during the Spanish-American War. After retiring in 1928, he lived to the ripe old age of forty-one years, three months and ten days. His stone reads:

Old Tom, Born 12 January 1892.
Entered the US Marine Corps 24 March 1894.
Retired US Marine Corps 30 March 1928.
Died 2 April 1933.

Served as mount for Col. William H. Huntington USMC in Cuba during
the war with Spain 1898. Semper Fidelis.

All of the cemeteries at the Portsmouth Naval Shipyard have restricted public access due to military security. Requests for a visitor's badge can be made through the shipyard.

Burial Grounds of York, Maine

Some of the eternal sleeping places of the residents of York, Maine, are still being discovered, adding to the chapters of history from one of the oldest towns in the state. In September 2018, a ground-penetrating radar survey was made of twenty-two thousand square feet of the First Parish Church Cemetery behind York Town Hall. A walk through the area by experts with a three-wheel cart and mapmaking software revealed eighty-nine unmarked graves in a burial ground that dates back two centuries. The identities of those who were buried there may never be known, as cemetery records are difficult to obtain and document.

The town of York does have a curious number of small burial grounds and historic family plots that can be found, from backyards to the side lots of major routes. From an unmarked grave hidden behind a stone wall next to the Cape Neddick Country Club to the edge of a driveway in the hills of the town, burials can be found around almost every bend of the road. It's hard to imagine what the area looked like when it was first settled, but using the burial grounds as a map to tell us about the community can be quite enlightening.

In 1641, a tract of land near the mouth of the York River on the southern coast of Maine, just three miles square, was incorporated by Sir Ferdinando Gorges. He was the original proprietor of the province of Maine, and the town was first referred to as Agamenticus and as Gorgeana, according to the Charter of 1642. The town was re-incorporated as York in 1652, when the province of Maine was annexed by the Massachusetts Bay Colony. The town grew quickly in the 1700s, relying largely on maritime trade, farming and fishing. Things declined briefly in the early 1800s but soon turned around as York was discovered to be a wonderful vacation destination for summer tourists. York has now become a year-round tourist destination, attracting visitors from far and near.

At the highest point in York, at the top of Mount Agamenticus, there is a legendary seventeenth-century grave site that still has people theorizing about its history. Two interpretive signs help to tell the story and separate fact from fiction:

Local folklore recounts the story of St. Aspinquid, as an Algonquin leader who converted to Christianity and preached for peace between European settlers and native tribes during the conflicts of the 17th century. Over the years, oral tradition has created many story lines that talk of the ultimate demise of St. Aspinquid in the Mt. Agamenticus area. One such story included an elaborate burial and celebration to honor his saintly qualities. The story was perpetuated in the 19th century as a romantic enticement to tourists who imitated a native tradition of placing a palm-sized rock on the summit in memory of St. Aspinquid and his struggle for peace. Over time these rocks accumulated to form a significant pile. Though the rock pile has been moved several times throughout the history of Mount Agamenticus, the tradition persists for Native Americans and continues to inspire a spiritual and reverent homage for the man who crossed cultures to bring peoples together.

The Native Americans of the Northeast believed the natural landscape was filled with spirits and supernatural forces. Their culture and survival was determined by the way they balanced both of their physical and spiritual worlds through prayers, songs, and ceremonies.

Some ceremonies required the construction of special structures made from stone. Many of them can still be seen today throughout the northeastern United States. These structures include cairns, chambers, niches, split stones, and pedestal or perched boulders.

Some cairns were created to honor a past event or an important person. Though this is not a burial site, the original mound at Mount Agamenticus may have been built to replicate a traditional Native American grave. Native Americans carry palm-sized stones from their homes to sites like this as a spiritual offering, to pay respect to their ancestors, or in memory of the land their ancestors occupied.

Another view of the legend can be found in *Charles Skinner's Myths and Legends of Our Own Land*, written in 1896:

> *The personality of Passaconaway, the powerful chief and prophet, is involved in doubt, but there can be no misprision of his wisdom. By some historians he has been made one with St. Aspenquid, the earliest of native missionaries among the Indians, who, after his conversion by French Jesuits, travelled from Maine to the Pacific, preaching to sixty-six tribes, healing the sick and working miracles, returning to die at the age of ninety-four. He was buried on the top of Agamenticus, Maine, where his manes were pacified with offerings of three thousand slain animals, and where his tombstone stood for a century after, bearing the legend, "Present, useful; absent, wanted; living, desired; dying, lamented."*

A pile of rocks surrounded by an oval stone circle stands between the signs, and from that vantage point, one can look toward the east over the Atlantic Ocean in the distance. It is frowned upon to place additional stones or mementos on the site, and there is some controversy regarding the location being moved from its original place in recent years.

One of the oldest common burying grounds in Maine, the graveyard of Old York Village (which is across from the current town hall) is steeped in local legends and lore. The burial ground was established around 1670, and the early grave markers were said to be simple wooden plank markers and fieldstones. Today, there are about 150 surviving gravestones, with the oldest dating from 1705. There are even a few gravestones that are carved "York, Massachusetts," reflecting back to the time before Maine became an official state and was no longer a province. A variety of winged skulls and death's heads can be found throughout the burial ground. Interments ended here in the late nineteenth century due to overcrowding. When you look at the grounds today, there appear to be many open areas without gravestones, where bodies are buried without markers. A keen eye looking at the ground can notice dips in the earth, where the coffins and graves have broken down and sank.

The gravestones have been meticulously cleaned and repaired in recent years, revealing the epitaphs and detailed carvings of the stones. In 2020, a large informational panel and map was constructed at the entrance to the burial ground by seventeen-year-old Tyson Mathews as an Eagle Scout project. The map details notable gravestones and helps to further interpret the burial ground for visitors.

A large stone marker near the road remembers the "hardy pioneers" who suffered through a disastrous Native American attack in the winter of 1692. This marks the spot in the burial ground where there is a mass grave for about forty people, including Shubael Dummer, the town's minister. Known as the Candlemas Raid, the unexpected assault was made early in the morning by upward of three hundred Abenaki Indians under the command of the French. At the end of the rampage, about eighty villagers were taken hostage and forced to walk to Canada. About one hundred York residents were dead. Many undefended homes had been burned to the ground, supplies and food destroyed and animals slaughtered. As the stone explains, many villagers also died on the long march to Canada. The result of this attack affected the settlement deeply, and it was also evident in the surviving children, as some who swore revenge for the cruel attack became fierce Indian fighters in their adult years. The memorial stone, placed on the site in the twentieth century by the Society for the Preservation of Historic Landmarks, is quite curious, as it is placed approximately where the mass grave is established, based on recollections of it being at the front and center of the grounds. The reasons behind the Candlemas Raid are still debated by some historians today.

The Old York Burial Ground offers a variety of gravestones telling many different stories of the people who are buried there.

One particular grave in the Old York Burial Ground stands out among the rest. A long stone slab lies on the ground behind a headstone. During any given visit, the slab is covered with coins, flowers, tokens, candles and jewelry charms. This site might be the most visited grave in the burial ground, and it certainly is one of the most legendary in the town. The headstone, carved in Boston by the Lamson family of stone carvers, is an incredibly dramatic portrait of a woman with two large eyes, stylized hair and a shroud around her shoulders. The stone, commissioned by Mary's husband, tells of his affections for his wife with a long and eloquent epitaph:

> *Here rests quite free from Life's*
> *Distressing Care,*
> *A loving wife*
> *A tender Parent dear;*
> *Cut down in the midst of days*
> *As you may see,*
> *But -stop- my grief;*
> *I soon shall equal be,*
> *When death shall stop my breath;*
> *And end my Time;*
> *God grant my Dust*
> *May mingle, then, with thine.*
> *Sacred to the memory of Mrs.*
> *Mary Nasson, wife of Mr. Samuel*
> *Nasson, who departed this life*
> *Augst. 28th. 1774*
> *Aetat 29.*

The legend (which has been around for nearly one hundred years) about the stone on the ground over the grave is quite a curious one; in fact, it is more unnerving in its truth. There are many varying accounts of the story of Mary Nasson, and in most of them is the notion that she practiced witchcraft in some form and that this was the reason for the manner of her burial. If we take a deeper look at the story, some of the misconceptions become building blocks for a captivating legend.

It was not uncommon for people to keep herbal cabinets and rooms in their homes in the eighteenth and nineteenth centuries. According to the story, Mary not only kept herbs, but she also knew how to use them well—just as good as, if not better than, some of the area doctors. Some

The portrait-style gravestone for Mary Nasson was carved in Boston, Massachusetts, by the Lamson family of stone carvers.

accounts allege that Mary would even perform the occasional exorcism. With all the mysterious activity surrounding Mary's life, some people thought that she might, in fact, be practicing witchcraft—an easy presumption for those who may have been superstitious.

When Mary passed away at the age of twenty-nine, a headstone, a footstone and a long stone slab were placed on her grave. Remarks by some people referred to the slab as the witch stone, designed to keep the "witch" from rising up out of the grave. It was also said that if you touched the headstone and then touched the slab, you could feel that the slab on the ground was warmer, owing to Mary's power rising up from the grave. Of course, there is a scientific explanation for the slab being warmer, as there is an opening in the grove of trees that allows the sun to shine down on the stone and warm it throughout the day. Perhaps some of the locals were too caught up in the legend to seek any other explanation. As far as the stone keeping Mary in the grave, that slab is actually called a "wolf stone." They are designed to keep animals from digging up the bodies in a burial ground. Wolf stones were quite common in many parts of New England and can still be found today. Not everyone was buried six feet under; it depended on the conditions of the grounds and the strength and will of the grave digger, among other factors. There are documented accounts from the town's church records that reveal that when the good folk of York left Sabbath services from the church across the street, they were more than once confronted with the gruesome spectacle of roaming hogs and cattle "well yoked and tinged as the law directs and allowed to go at large" rooting bodies up from fresh burials.

There is a fascinating drawing of the burial ground in the collection of the Old York Historical Society that was done in the 1830s. The drawing, made by an older resident of York, was based on his childhood memory of the burial ground and actually shows the cemetery with multiple wolf stones on the graves. There is some discussion that as the cemetery became abandoned

A variety of gifts and offerings is strewn across the legendary "witch stone" that covers Mary Nasson's grave.

and disused, perhaps the locals went in and removed the stones to be used as part of foundations and other structures, as the threat of rooting animals in an overgrown burial ground didn't seem an issue any longer. In addition, there is the theory that the low, original stone wall around the burial was raised with the wolf stones placed on top.

In the 1894 book *Ancient City of Gorgeana and Modern Town of York (Maine) from Its Earliest Settlement* by George Alexander Emery, there is a commentary on the burial of Mary Nasson, arguing that she couldn't have been a witch because she died too young and it was known that witches seldom or never married. In addition, the passage goes on the say that "it would have been very doubtful, indeed, if the powers that were would have allowed, or even, suffered, her burial in the grave-yard. If a witch, she would have been interred in the 'rough sands of the sea, at low-water mark, where the tide ebbs and flows twice in twenty-four hours,' or on a highway, at the junction of three roads."

Whether or not you choose to believe that Mary was a witch, there is also the legend of her spirit wandering the burial ground. There are stories that bunches of wildflowers (posies) can be found along the stone wall as gifts for children. Many paranormal groups and amateur ghost investigators claim that they have captured photos of light anomalies and unexplained phenomena in the area of her grave from just outside the grounds. Could the spirit of Mary Nasson be making herself known as a sweet and kindly spirit, or are they just additional stories to add to the centuries-old legend? You decide.

The purple slate headstone and footstone marking Lucy Moodey's burial place remind visitors of how fragile life was in early New England. A rare sentiment found on gravestones from this time, the word *RESURRECTION* reads in bold letters, reflecting the purity and innocence of a newborn child who died the same day she was born. The remainder of the stone reads:

> *To Immortality in Spotless Beauty with all other*
> *Bodily Perfections after the fashion of Christ's*
> *Glorious Body is expected for*
> *the sub adjacent dust of Lucy Moodey*
> *who was born and died, July the 6 1705.*
> *Thus Birth, Spousals to Christ, Death, Coronation*
> *All in One day may have their Celebration.*

The gravestone for Elizabeth Hyslop is a reminder that even during a visit with friends, one might be spirited away to the other side:

> *In Memory of*
> *Mrs. Elizabeth*
> *wife of David Hyslop*
> *of Brookline*
> *who died suddenly*
> *when on a visit to*
> *her friends*
> *June AD 1808*
> *Aged 46 yrs.*

The gravestone for Mrs. Lucy Sewall offers a lengthy epitaph, which prompts one to be reminded that gravestone carvers typically charged by the letter, so the longer the epitaph the higher the price to be remembered by:

In Memory of
Mrs. Lucy Sewall
wife of Mr. Storer Sewall
daughter of Col. J. Moulton
who departed this life Jan. 14. 1800
in the 43d year of her age.

Blessed shade! Thy life is not measured by age nor thy memory by death. Thou still livest on the tongue of friendship & charity. Thy praise full glows in the heart of conjugal & filial tenderness. The bosom of an affectionate husband & the tears of an orphan shall perpetuate the remembrance of thee till our kindred souls unite in those realms where pain & sorrow never affect.

The trees in the burial ground are worthy of note, as a closer examination will reveal that many of them have small, silver discs that have numbers stamped on them. The trees are monitored and surveyed in regards to their health and growth. There has been a large grove of sassafras trees growing for a number of years on the grounds. These are some of the tallest sassafras trees in New England, towering over all of the other ancient trees that stand here. The lore behind the trees is quite curious and relevant to the story of the early settlers in the area. One of the first things some explorers to the New World searched for was sassafras, as it was thought to be an elixir of life and a healer of several ills. The leaves were used to make healing balms, tinctures and ointments, and the roots were used for sassafras tea for internal ailments. It is an interesting observation that these majestic trees have been thriving, with their roots digging into the depths of the burial ground. In 2014, a microburst tore through the village and took down thirteen of the sassafras trees in the burial ground; amazingly, not a single gravestone was damaged. Today, there is still evidence of that devastating storm that rattled the town, with several tree stumps visible throughout the burial ground.

A final lingering legend about the burial ground is the appearance of shadow people wandering between the gravestones at night. There are reports of interesting phenomena happening around the burial ground on summer and autumn nights, with everything from bats feeding on mosquitos to owls hooting to one another. A distant look at the gravestones as they cast long shadows across the grounds reveals what could look like a head and shoulders due to the shape of the curved tops. Is the appearance of disembodied shadows all a trick of the eye? Could it be the imagination or something more? Perhaps a visit at dusk under a full moon will reveal the answer.

LOUGEE-FOSS-MUDGETT CEMETERY, PARSONSFIELD

Gilman Lougee was the deacon of the First Church in Parsonsfield, and he lived in a log house at the bottom of Mudgett's Hill. Admired for his apple trees that were still bearing bountiful fruit over one hundred years after his death. One of his grave markers is most unusual. One day, while working in a clay pit, a large rock fell and killed him when he was just thirty-five years old. It is that same exact rock that was carved into and placed on his grave. It reads: "Dea. G. Lougee killed by this stone September 1788." He has a tall slate marker on his grave as well.

LAUREL HILL CEMETERY, SACO, MAINE

Laurel Hill Cemetery is the definition of a tranquil and serene garden-style cemetery. Established in 1844, the cemetery started out as a small group of eighteenth-century graves, and the current cemetery, slowly and quite beautifully, was established around it. From rows of cherry blossom trees in the spring to brilliant Japanese maple leaves in the fall, the cemetery is inviting for those who are looking for a peaceful, quiet place to walk among gravestones, beautiful statuary and nature.

The cemetery connects to the shore of the Saco River with fields of tens of thousands of daffodils in the spring. This sea of vibrant yellow flowers brings a beauty and cheerful nature tumbling down to the tall marsh grasses inhabited by birds of all kinds that call this area their home. Paths seemingly disappear off into the trees, but grave markers both tall and small can be seen by keen eyes. A small section of infant graves with metal markers dating back to the 1960s and 1970s can be found along one of those trails.

Family plots surrounded by ornately fashioned ironwork shaped into leaves and branches take shape across the landscape. One family plot even has iron fingers on the posts pointing skyward to reflect the ascension to heaven. Three stone steps can be found at the entrances to other plots with

Left: Tens of thousands of daffodils can be found on the hillside in the spring at the back of Laurel Hill Cemetery in Saco.

Below: The chapel at the Laurel Hill Cemetery was built in 1890.

family names, welcoming visitors to step up into the realm of faith, hope and love. Toward the front of the cemetery is a Queen Anne–style chapel that was built in 1890 and still serves for both funerals and weddings.

A white marble gravestone for Charles Edwin Burbank reads:

> *Charles Edwin*
> *only son of James M. & Phebe H. Burbank*
> *Died*
> *Oct. 26, 1855*
> *Aged 18 years, 8 mos. & 8 days*
> *Weep not for me my kindred dear*
> *I am not dead but slumber here,*
> *Dry up your tears they're all in vain*
> *We only part to meet again.*

One might wonder why adding the additional details of months and days to the age of a deceased person is necessary to their epitaph. In a tradition that could also be found in colonial America, it was often important to include these details of age to illustrate to belief of making the most of every moment on earth—that we are not guaranteed a certain time and that each day is a treasure.

There are several Maine congressmen who are buried in the cemetery, as well as service veterans going back nearly two hundred years. A tall obelisk marks the grave of John Fairfield, who served as the governor of Maine. He was born in Saco and served four terms from 1838 to 1843. One of his many claims to fame happened when his friend Congressman Jonathan Cilley was killed in a duel with William Graves, a representative from Kentucky. John Fairfield demanded a full investigation into the incident, and it was considered quite controversial to bring the matter before Congress; because of his efforts, dueling was outlawed in the District of Columbia. John suffered an untimely death at the age of fifty on December 24, 1847, in Washington, D.C. He had been suffering from knee pain that never quite healed despite several operations. The doctor who treated him the final time injected a copper sulfate solution into his leg while he drained the pressure. The solution was not drained in time, and it was absorbed into his nervous system, causing further paralysis and leading to his death.

A modern columbarium can be found on the grounds with carved mountains and detailed nature scenes, along with uplifting sentiments such as "I have come to the end of the road, the Lord has taken me. You need not weep for me anymore, why cry for a soul set free. Miss me a little, but not too long. And not with your head held low. Remember the joy of the love we shared. Miss me, but let me go."

OLEA BULL VAUGHN, SHAPLEIGH CEMETERY, WEST LEBANON, MAINE

In the Shapleigh Cemetery, located on Shapleigh Road in West Lebanon, there is an unusually large urn with the name Olea Bull Vaughn on it. This is an identical urn to one for her father, Ole Bull, which is located in a cemetery in Bergen, Norway. Ole was hailed as one of the greatest violinists of his era and was a musical prodigy. When he died in 1880, Norway held a Day of National Mourning in his honor.

Olea was born in Wisconsin, and her mother, Sara, a pianist, and father toured the United States and Europe performing concerts together. Olea grew up with the Shapleigh family in West Lebanon and married Henry Goodwin Vaughn on February 5, 1894. Sara died in January 1911, and the newspapers from Boston, Massachusetts, to Alfred, Maine, covered the story of the court dispute over Olea's mother's will. The headlines hinted at a scandal over the terms of the will. The terms included scattering her mother's ashes over her father's grave in Norway and, worst of all, no share of any sort of inheritance.

The urn on Olea Bull's grave is identical to the one on her father's grave in Bergen, Norway.

The court records alleged estrangement, and Olea suggested that her mother was not of sound mind and good judgment. The testimony was sensational, as was some of the evidence. A piece of correspondence between mother and daughter given to the judge to consider was a horoscope commissioned for Olea by her mother. The horoscope was written by a New York astrologist who was her mother's friend and was into the occult and psychics. Olea was concerned about the family's reputation when it was revealed that her mother claimed to have visions of her deceased father and grandmother.

The legal wrangling over the $500,000 fortune went on for about a month in court. Finally, in a twist no one could have anticipated, Olea died from tuberculosis the morning of the court's decision. The judge ruled in her favor, granting her almost the entire estate. Olea was forty years old when she died just four months after her mother. The question then became: who was going to benefit from the court's decision? Olea had a daughter, Edwina, who had passed away as a young child. Trying to heal her grief, she adopted three children from an orphanage in Boston: Sylvia, Dorothy and David. Her substantial estate went to her children and attorney, Mr. Bartlett. Her Boston friends boarded a train to attend her funeral in West Lebanon on July 20, 1911, to pay their final respects to Olea.

PORTLAND STREET CEMETERY, SOUTH BERWICK, MAINE

MISSING
You walked beside me, quick and free;
With lingering touch you grasped my hand;
Your eyes looked laughingly in mine;
And now—I can not understand.
I long for you, I mourn for you,
Through all the dark and lonely hours.
Heavy the weight the pallmen lift,
And cover silently with flowers.
—Sarah Orne Jewett

Both of Sarah Orne Jewett's parents were highly educated, and her first published article in the *Atlantic Monthly* came out while she was still a schoolgirl (under a pseudonym). In 1901, she received the degree of Doctor of Letters from Bowdoin College. Receiving many literary honors, she lyrically wrote about rural life, sometimes writing an average of nine thousand words per day. She was described as a charming woman, quiet and reserved, with a low voice, and possessing a fine sense of humor and charm. She was a friend to Mark Twain, and one of her most popular books offered a look at perspectives on a changing community. *The Country of the Pointed Firs* told compassionate stories of Mainers, exploring their traditions, folkways and personalities.

A lilac bush hangs over the grave for Sarah Orne Jewett, just as she wished.

In a 1901 interview, she explained that she wanted to give a proper explanation of interpreting the country people of her native state. She wanted to teach the world that country people were not the awkward, ignorant creatures that many had misinterpreted them to be. It was Sarah's wish to have people know the grand, simple lives of fellow Mainers. "I was born here and I hope to die here, leaving the lilac bushes still green and all the chairs in their places," she said.

She became an established author and had many notable visitors to her house, such as Edith Wharton and Willa Cather. Much of Sarah's material for her books was drawn from her hometown of South Berwick, Maine. Her favorite story of hers, "The Country Doctor," was a tribute to the career of her father, who was for many years a practitioner beloved by hundreds of grateful patients in the region. An independent, free-thinking woman, Sarah never married or had children, but instead seemed dedicated to her writing.

On the evening of June 24, 1909, she passed away after a long illness that had caused both a stroke and paralysis of one side of her body. Described

The stack of marble books for each member of the Libbey family is very unique, and each is beautifully crafted.

as still having a clear mind and physically helpless, she was fifty-nine years old when she passed away. Her 1774 Georgian-style house is available to be visited in season and is operated by Historic New England. There are several exhibits that help tell Sarah's story, and her desk is at the front end of the second-floor hall, overlooking downtown, as it was when she lived and wrote there. Her bedroom looks essentially as it did at the time of her death. The final resting place for Sarah can be found just down the road at the Portland Street Cemetery. In the spring, blue wildflowers bloom along the edges of her table stone, and in the summer it's shaded by the neighboring lilac bush. The inscription on the tablet reads:

> *To the dear memory of*
> *SARAH ORNE JEWETT*
> *Daughter of Doctor Theodore H. and Caroline F. Jewett*
> *Born the third of September 1849*
> *Died the twenty fourth of June 1909*
> *Until the day breaks and the shadows flee away.*

In the far western corner of the cemetery, there is a large monument that, perhaps, Sarah Orne Jewett would have found interesting, as it is a large stack of books carved out of marble. This towering monument has an angel standing on top, pointing skyward. A closer look at the books reveals names on the spines along with some short sentiments. This marker for the Libbey family tells the story of Mark and his wife, Eliza, who had six children—all of them died young except for one, who lived into adulthood. "Blessed Be" and "Beloved Sleep" are carved on the memorial. Mark was treasurer for the Town of South Berwick, and he sold bicycles. His son, Mark Addison, was quite an inventor and was mechanically gifted. He built an indoor skating rink in town, taught at the Massachusetts Institute of Technology and even designed a scale model of a car he came up with. This incredible monument is completely one of a kind among the cemeteries of Maine.

HATCH CEMETERY—KENNEBUNK, MAINE

Traveling along Route 95 North in Kennebunk, Maine, many people don't expect to see a burial ground at the edge of the breakdown lane. Thousands of people every day travel along a modern road that crosses what used to be a family farm. The area that the cemetery sits in was referred to as early as 1732 as the Cat Mousam District, and a nearby sawmill was known as the Cat Mill. In fact, the present Cat Mousam Road (now the Sanford Road) was opened for travel in 1778.

Obediah Hatch lived at the time of Paul Revere and Daniel Boone (both of whom were born in 1735), and he was a greatly respected man who was the deacon in the Second Parish Church of Wells. Hatch built his first house near the mill, across from the river, and a few years later, he tore that house down and built a larger one north of the original location. Obediah and his wife, Jerusha, had six children, and he died at the age of eighty-nine on November 23, 1819. There are believed to be nineteen people buried in the yard, including Hannah Mitchell, who was widowed when her husband, John Hatch (Obediah's and Jerusha's son), died while trying to cross the river. Hannah remarried a man named James Mitchell, which accounts for the Mitchell family also being buried at the cemetery. According to records, Hannah is buried between her first and second husband. The last burial to take place was in 1883, believed to be that of Eunice Littlefield.

In 1948, when the interstate was new, the little cemetery made headlines as a reminder of the smaller settlements that used to dot York County. Once again in 2002, when the highway was being widened, there was quite a bit of concern regarding what was going to happen to the cemetery. The area around the cemetery was cleaned and cleared, and a protective guardrail was installed; during the winter, a temporary chain link fence was installed to add additional protection during snowplow season. On Veterans Day and Memorial Day, flags are still placed in the cemetery; however, officials remind people who are interested in pulling over for a visit that doing so is not only unsafe but also illegal. When passing along on the highway, a glimpse in the rear-view mirror reveals to us our past, which is sometimes closer than we realize.

Kittery Point Cemetery

Old Burying Ground, sometimes referred to as the Kittery Point Cemetery, was established in 1714. Across the street, the First Congregational Church in Kittery Point, which was built in 1731, is the oldest church building still standing in Maine. Records tell us that in 1733, it was voted to build a stone wall around the cemetery. In the nineteenth century, burial lots were

The Kittery Point Cemetery is located at a bend in the road and overlooks the Piscataqua River.

two dollars apiece, with the stipulation that enough dirt be brought to cover the casket.

Reverend Benjamin Stevens became the minister at the church in 1751, and he died rather suddenly in 1791. Reverend Samuel Haven of South Church in Portsmouth preached the funeral sermon. He came by boat, and "the shore was lined with boats, and the meeting house filled to overflowing with a weeping multitude," according to Reverend Miller. Stevens's gravestone is inscribed as follows:

> *In memory of the Rev'd Benjamin Stevens D D Pastor of the First Church in Kittery, who departed this life in the joyful hope of a better, May ye 18th 1791: in the 71st year of his age and 41st of his ministry.*

> *In him, the Gentleman, the Scholar, the grave divine, the cheerful Christian, the affectionate, charitable & laborious Pastor, the faithful friend & the tender Parent were happily united.*

> *This grave contains the feeble mould'ring clay,*

> *The Spirit triumphs in Eternal day.*

Levi Lincoln Thaxter, who died on May 31, 1884, at the age of sixty, is also buried here. A Harvard-educated lawyer, Levi was also known for his readings of poetry by Robert Browning, a famous Victorian English poet. In tribute, Robert Browning reportedly penned an original epitaph when Levi died. Levi was also the husband of poetess Celia Thaxter, who lived on nearby Appledore Island (part of the Isles of Shoals). Before Celia died ten years later in 1894, she chose to be buried at the Laighton family cemetery on the island.

The original epitaph written for Levi by Robert Browning can be found on the boulder that serves as his grave marker:

> *Thou, whom these eyes saw never; say friends true who say my soul, helped onward by my song, though all unwittingly, has helped thee too? I gave of but the little that I knew; how were the gift requited, while along life's path I pace, couldst thou make weakness strong; help me with knowledge—for life's old, death's new.*

One of the most striking grave markers in the cemetery recalls the shipwreck of the brig *Hattie Eaton*. It was during a March 1876 storm that

Left: The gravestone for John Walker displays a winged skull, sometimes referred to as a death's head, which is a common motif found throughout New England from the seventeen and early eighteenth centuries.

Right: The detailed carving on the memorial stone for the shipwreck of the *Hattie Eaton* reveals the ship running aground on jagged rocks.

the ship was driven into rocky outcropping of Gerrish Island. The ship had recently left Boston on its way to Cuba with a cargo of sugar and molasses; the only survivor of the wreck was the first mate. The story, offered in the *Boston Post* newspaper, offered a grim eyewitness account of the wreck:

> *B. Mitchell, who lives in the nearest house, saw the vessel coming in, and hastened to the beach to render any possible assistance. She came like a race horse…she struck two rocks, a little more than her length from shore: the captain sprang into the fore rigging and ran aloft to the top mast, when he entwined himself in the rigging to prevent being jerked overboard, while the rest of the crew stuck to the deck. The heavy sea soon swung the vessel around so that her bow was out to sea and the stern toward the land, at the same time careening her so that the masts were nearly parallel with the water, bringing the captain close down to a ledge of rock not far from the shore. Mr. Mitchell ran for the ledge in the belief that he could help the man*

in the rigging, but on getting there he could he could not reach him by about eight feet. The poor fellow begged earnestly for aid, but the boiling surf cut off all help. The doomed man, soon after, seeing the hopelessness of the situation, gave Mr. Mitchell his name and the name of the vessel. Suddenly a huge sea struck the wreck and rolled the mast under the water, the captain rolling under with it, never to appear again as a living man. One colored man stripped himself, plunged overboard and struggles desperately to reach the shore; but though he was a powerful swimmer he was but as a feather in the surf, which repeatedly bore him close in to the rocks only to sweep him a hundred feet away in another moment, and at last dashed him against a rock with a force that must instantly have crushed out his life. One man [the mate] was still alive, holding on near the foremast, the bow of the vessel being still intact and the after part much shattered.

The captain of the *Hattie Eaton,* James Cook of East Boston, Massachusetts, was thirty-nine years old and was described to be a "very worthy and highly respected shipmaster" who left behind a wife and two children. Oddly, when his body washed ashore, his watch was recovered, and it had stopped at 3:25 p.m., which was considered the exact time of the wreck. In 1941, a memorial stone was commissioned and installed in the cemetery:

Brig "Hattie Eaton"
W.I. to Boston
Cast away on Gerrish
Island Mch 21, 1876
Crew of 8 white and
negro and 1 stowaway,
Near this stone lie six
bodies never claimed.

The gravestone for Margaret Hills tells another story of maritime danger, when she and her husband, Oliver, died by drowning on their passage from Belfast, Maine, to Boston, Massachusetts:

Consort of Oliver Hills died Oct 31st 1803 ae 28.
I lost my life in the raging seas:
A Sovereign God does as he please—
My Kittery friends they did appear
And my remains they buried here.

The gravestone for Robert Cutt Whipple is dated 1761, and it has a pair of angels under a crown, a symbol of the "Great Awakening" where death was a reunion with those who had gone before.

This scenic cemetery along the shore of the Piscataqua River, at a historic bend in the road, is well maintained and has an excellent variety of gravestones reflecting the names of those who lived and passed through the oldest town in Maine. Visitors can also view the 1760 Georgian mansion known as the Lady Pepperell House, which is adjacent to the cemetery.

GREATER PORTLAND
AND CASCO BAY

Governor Baxter Pet Cemetery, Mackworth Island, Casco Bay

On June 1, 1923, the flag at the Maine Statehouse was lowered to half-staff in respect to the memory of Garry, the faithful dog friend and almost constant companion of Governor Percival P. Baxter. Garry, an Irish setter whose predecessors were in the governor's family for thirty-seven consecutive years, was laid to rest on Mackworth Island. The island was the location of the summer home for Governor Baxter, who was a dog lover and breeder of Irish setters. He had established a burial ground for fourteen of his dogs and one horse. The gravestone on the island for his horse reads:

> *Jerry Roan, A Noble Horse and a Kind Friend.*
> *Died Mar. 1, 1904, AEt. 35 years.*

A wooden sign erected in the burial ground once read:

> *The State of Maine by legislative Act, Chapter 1, Laws of 1943, Accepted the gift of Mackworth Island and covenanted to maintain forever this burial place of my dogs with the stone wall and boulder with the bronze marker thereon erected to their memory, Percival P. Baxter.*

In 1957, the state converted his home into the Baxter School for the Deaf, which remains open to this day. Governor Baxter died at the age of ninety-two in 1969, and his ashes were scattered throughout Baxter State Park, which he established and left a trust to maintain. The pet cemetery on Mackworth Island can be easily visited by following the walking trail around the outer edge of the island. The wooden sign no longer remains; however, the gravestones and memorials with the names of Governor Baxter's dogs are still there surrounded by fieldstone walls.

Western Cemetery—Portland, Maine

The Western Cemetery is described in the 1876 book *Portland and Vicinity* by Edward Henry Elwell as "lying on the slope of Bramhall's Hill within the limits of the city, comprises about fifteen acres and was laid out in 1829." The cemetery remained was the city's primary burying ground until 1852 when the garden-style Evergreen Cemetery opened. It is estimated that there are 6,600 marked and unmarked graves throughout the grounds. In 1881, the cost of interments in the cemetery for adults was $2.00 and children were $1.50. The main entrance, the 1914 Davis Memorial Gate, was designed by John Calvin Stevens.

The cemetery is located in the city's Western Promenade area, and the neighboring streets are lined with grand mansions and elegant homes, most built in the late Victorian era. During the cemetery's early days, many families had their relatives' remains moved here from smaller plots throughout the city. Buried here are such distinguished residents as Portland's greatest capitalist, John Bundy Brown, and the family of Henry Wadsworth Longfellow. One of the most conspicuous monuments here is that of Chief Justice Prentiss Mellen, erected in 1850 by the state bar association.

Given the cemetery's apparently favorable location, it is surprising to discover that the grounds have suffered from neglect and severe vandalism over the years. A walk through the cemetery reveals an alarming number of broken gravestones, with the top halves stacked up or leaned against the pitch pine trees. At the height of summer, many family plots disappear under tall grasses that camouflage all traces of gravestones. From July 1988 to August 1989, the city of Portland experienced one of the most severe episodes of vandalism in its cemeteries: 1,943 gravestones were vandalized or destroyed, and about 1,000 of those were in the Western Cemetery. The

Looking across a section of broken gravestones, you can see some of the magnificent homes that surround the Western Cemetery.

Are there secrets hidden in some of the tombs of the Western Cemetery?

perpetrators were eventually caught; however, most of the gravestones have not been replaced or even repaired.

From the entrance to the graveyard along the walking path to the right there is a wall of tombs. One of the most noticeable names is Longfellow. This granite tomb was built into the hillside behind the stately mansions, and over the years, many people have wondered what—or who—was inside. One of the most widely read American poets, Henry Wadsworth Longfellow was born in Portland, Maine, and he often returned for frequent visits. Although he is buried at the famous Mount Auburn Cemetery in Cambridge, Massachusetts, according to records, his parents, two brothers and other relatives were laid to rest in the Western Cemetery tomb.

During restoration work in 1986, it was written in a *Portland Press Herald* newspaper article that the tomb was discovered to be completely empty. This surprising revelation had been made while workers were replacing the brick that sealed the tomb entrance closed. Some people speculated that the bodies had been moved to the Evergreen Cemetery in Portland, yet there are no records available to confirm that. Further research notes that the remains were not moved to Duxbury, Massachusetts, where the family also had ties.

One theory is that the remains are hidden behind a secret wall in the tomb, although there has been no definitive proof of this. The reasoning behind that theory is that perhaps Anne Longfellow Pierce (who was the last occupant of the Longfellow House on Congress Street) had reason to believe the tomb would be vandalized and therefore safeguarded the bodies behind an inner wall of the tomb. Today, by all outward appearances, the tomb appears to be mysteriously empty.

Traveling the winding paths in the cemetery will eventually lead visitors to the large Irish American section of burials. Many immigrants came to Portland during the late nineteenth and twentieth centuries. There is even a monument that memorializes those who died in the potato famine of 1845–49. The sturdy stones that still remain in this area have wonderfully detailed Celtic designs, carvings and sentiments.

Uncertainty surrounds the burial location of Lieutenant Robert E. Allen Jr., as there are conflicting reports of where he is buried. According to the Maine Veterans Cemetery records, he was interred at the Evergreen Cemetery; however, according to the Western Cemetery record, he was buried at the Western. There is no gravestone for him at either location. Lieutenant Allen died at the age of twenty-one, and there is some documentation that has survived to tell his story in a book called *American Patriotism*, which was written in 1869 by Leonard Brown:

He enlisted as a private in Company D, May 4, 1861 at the age of twenty. He received promotion to the office of First Lieutenant in the 1st U.S. Cavalry, Army of the Potomac. [He] was wounded June 1, 1862 at the battle of Fair Oaks. Being left on the field, he fell into the hands of the enemy and, and was carried to Richmond [Virginia]. The rebel surgeons amputated his leg, the bone being badly shattered. After lying in [the] hospital for a short time he was exchanged and sent to New York. There it was found necessary to again amputate his limb. From the effects of these repeated operations he did not recover—death occurring to him before his relatives knew of his exchange.

He loved the profession of arms, coveted a position in the regular service. His father had marked out for him a different course in life and would not give him any encouragement in the way that Robert's own heart was set upon. But Robert being active and persevering, well educated, intelligent, and of soldierly appearance, was not long in finding friends to make his wished known to the proper authorities. Proud to be always at his post of duty, honorable and brave, he doubtless would have risen to high command, but for being ordered otherwise. An accomplished scholar, a good mathematician, and master of the French language, there was not in our army a young man of greater intelligence and promise.

It is unfortunate that the remains of this promising soldier have been misplaced; how many other veterans lie in unmarked or illegible graves at the Western Cemetery?

IT SEEMS AS THOUGH people really do have a fascination with the folklore of witches and vampires, but some stories are just long-told urban legends without any basis in fact. A visit to a particular grave in the Western Cemetery could almost convince a person that there is some sort of ritual happening there. Rows of sparkling amethyst and quartz crystals are carefully stacked up on stones in some strange mystical order. The grave marker itself is rather intriguing, as it looks like an ornate coffin, with a long cross and Celtic knot work carved on it. Broken gravestones surround the large central grave. The remains of what used to be a stone cross now lie in a heap at the head of the grave.

There are few remaining letters on the stone, as much has crumbled away and is completely illegible. In part, what can be seen reads:

Requiem Aeternam (Eternal Rest)
Dona ei Domine (Grant Unto Them)
Et lux perpetua (Let Perpetual Light)
Luceat eis. (Shine Upon Them)

Via crucis (The Path of Suffering)
Via lucis (The Way of Light)

O vos…(Rest)
Orame pro Anima (Pray for the Soul)
O Johannis W.C. Baker (of John WC Baker)
Diaconi qui namus (Deacon of virtue)
Jan. 13, 1837—Feb. 1, 1871

Reverend John White Chickering Baker died at the age of thirty-four on his voyage from England to America, and his grave marker was carved to look similar to the coffin in which he was interred. As the dramatically

People are intrigued by the legends and folklore of one particular grave at the Western Cemetery.

designed gravestone disintegrated, the legend grew about people being unable to walk by without leaving an offering to the "witch" or "vampire" that is buried there. Over the years, I have personally met many people who have asked about the "witch story" related to this grave. Imagine their surprise when they found out who was really buried here.

Webster Cemetery, Freeport, Maine

Buried in the humble Webster Cemetery, just a few miles from one of the most successful Maine companies that bears his name, is Leon Leonwood Bean, also known as L.L. Bean. His ingenuity and love for the outdoors came together in one of the most famous stories to come out of Maine. His name became known to hunters and fishermen around the world for the inventiveness of his uniquely designed Maine hunting shoe to keep their feet dry. A mail-order catalogue full of clothing, sportsmen equipment and thousands of other useful items built L.L. Bean's empire. Some of his most famous customers included boxing's Jack Dempsey and baseball's Ted Williams. Bean was the type of person whom everyone felt they knew through the products he offered and the work that he did.

L.L. Bean was born quite humbly in Greenwood, Maine, in 1872 and was the son of a Yankee horse trader; when he was twelve, both of his parents died within days of each other. With some schooling and a good business course under his belt, along with trial and error, he committed to a good product, leading to a U.S. patent and success. With a solid entrepreneurial sensibility, he strived to make a good idea even better, and with a 100 percent money-back guarantee, he sold enough boots by 1918 to open up a twenty-four-hour business in Freeport, Maine. He was known for saying in reference to his boots in the L.L. Bean catalogue that "a man might like them better than his wife."

Putting his enthusiasm as a sportsman into a book, L.L. Bean authored *Hunting, Fishing and Camping* (1942) and his autobiography, *My Story: The Autobiography of a Down-East Merchant* (1960), both of which were quite successful. He died on February 5, 1967, at the age of ninety-four in Pompano Beach, Florida. His obituary in the *Boston Globe* included a colorful description of his Freeport factory, "which appears a combination of Grandma's attic and a roller coaster that knew better days." Bean wasn't interested in new technology or moving his factory out of Maine.

The gravestone of L.L. Bean can be found at the Webster Cemetery, which is about a ten-minute drive from the location of the L.L. Bean store.

The Maine Medical Center in Portland, Maine, named one of its wings in his honor, and his portrait hangs in a ground-floor corridor at the hospital. His simple granite gravestone can be found between two evergreen bushes, which are symbols of eternal life and can thrive even during the coldest months of the year.

OLD HARPSWELL COMMON BURIAL GROUND

The town of Harpswell, Maine, was officially settled in the late 1600s and incorporated in 1758, and it is situated on a quiet but dramatic peninsula that reaches into Casco Bay. The community is connected by a series of bridges crisscrossing a series of charming islands with a deep fishing heritage. You can almost imagine the steamer boats coming in full of summer residents along the docks and the sounds of the Pinkham delivery wagon going by, full of everything from meats to confections. These days,

Near the entrance to the Old Common Cemetery in Harpswell are granite posts with horse tie-ups.

traveling into the villages of Harpswell, one might discover a number of artisan handicrafts sold right out of the homes and barns of the makers, such as quilts, paintings and pottery.

Approaching the Old Common Cemetery in Harpswell, a broad, lichen-covered stone wall marks the boundary behind tall granite posts that were once used as horse ties for the old First Parish Meetinghouse, which still stands at the entrance to the grounds. The meetinghouse is a registered historic landmark and was constructed between 1757 and 1759. Amazingly, the meetinghouse is so valued by the National Association of Architects that twelve blueprints were files with the National Archives in Washington, D.C., so that the building could be re-created if it were ever destroyed. The dramatic interior of the meetinghouse features a ten-foot-high pulpit and sounding board, as well as pumpkin pine pews.

If you visit the cemetery in the spring, you will discover thousands of lily of the valley flowers blooming along the entrance and edging the perimeter. Lily of the valley has been used as a symbol of resurrection throughout time, especially on gravestone art. The trees can be seen while looking toward the back of the burial ground—young but densely situated.

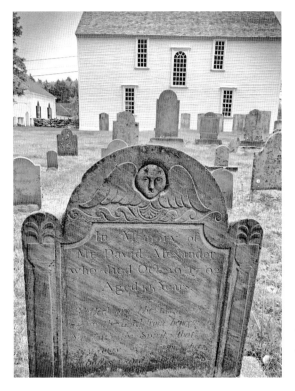

The 1792 gravestone for David Alexander is one of many stones that has been repaired at the cemetery.

In 2001, the town began a major renovation and restoration to the graveyard, clearing away brush and overgrown grasses. As part of the refurbishment, the town straightened and cleaned many of the gravestones, making some readable once again. The oldest readable stone was placed in the ground sometime around 1758, while earlier wooden markers have been lost to time and the elements. The quality and variety of the carvings and some very lyrical epitaphs create a reflective atmosphere in this welcoming place. The cemetery was in use until about 1900, when it became necessary to refuse further interments because old graves were being uncovered whenever a new grave was dug.

There are many stones that record the names of the early settlers throughout the grounds. The variety of epitaphs will keep the curious reading throughout their visit to the burial ground:

In Memory of Miss Elizabeth Eaton
Who Exchanged Worlds
January 13, 1806, Age 65
Those active limbs in this cold grave are laid,

Which I possest & to have natured paid,
That debt you owe & soon you must repay
Prepare for death & the great rising day

There is a wonderful collection of eighteenth- and nineteenth-century funerary art, including a young angel riding on billowy clouds, pointing skyward to the heavens, and a hand reaching through the clouds plucking a tender rosebud from a bush. An intricately carved cherub wears an elaborate headdress on one stone, and there is a variety of winged skulls, cherubs and funerary urns. Peeking carved suns disappear below the horizon line on several stones to symbolize the end of life.

One particularly sad epitaph is for little Freeman Allen:

Freeman M. Allen
Son of Elisha & Jane
March 29, 1851
Aged 2 years, 6 months
Our infant baby, the smiling boy
Its father's hope, its mother's joy
In three years resigned its breath
His sparkling eyes are boxed in death.

A small marble stone marks the grave of baby Oliver, who was born and died the same day, November 10, 1879. The stone for Hugh Alexander, dated 1807, describes how he "Bid adieu to time" in hopes of a "Glorious resurrection." The marker for Margaret Bishop, who died in 1862, reads: "Dear Mother! We can ne'er forget. The farewell gaze, the tender sigh. Thy parting words so full of love, When gathered round to see thee die."

Goodwife Hannah Stover is buried somewhere unknown in the burial ground in an unmarked grave. Stover was a Quaker, and she caused a great deal of scandal among the non-Quaker congregation by refusing to be present at the services in the old square church. There were rumors throughout the village of her having a wilder and darker character. She was originally from neighboring Freeport, and many people in town scorned her for being a witch.

There were some accusations of Hannah's witch wiles by some of the fishermen, who claimed that she had cursed everything from their cows to fishing nets and the sails on their boats. There was one woman who claimed that Hannah had bewitched her husband, Elkniah, and that he could not see her witchy ways.

When Hannah died, the men of Harpswell Neck refused to carry her coffin to the meetinghouse for a Christian burial. Believing her to be a good person, the fishermen's wives went against their husbands' wishes and carried the coffin to the burial ground instead. Upon their arrival, on a cold, dreary November morning, the wives ran into an angry mob, led by Ezra Johnston, and a commotion at the gates of the burial ground commenced. Wild accusations filled the air, insisting that Hannah was a witch and should not be interred in the burial ground. An argument between Parson Eaton, one of the wives and an angry Ezra Johnston ensued. He relayed the following accusation:

> *Last Sabbath night I was awoken in my sleep to the British bark off the point, and dragged by the Devil's imps up and down the sides till I was bruised and aching in every bones of my body. And I might have been killed but that daylight drew on, and with my own ears I heard Goodwife Stover say: "Let him go; 'tis almost cock-crowing." I knew her voice as well as I know my own, and that but two days before she died.*

Mercy Stover, Hannah's stepdaughter, and Goody Cole spoke up and reminded the townspeople of Hannah's kindness and the unwavering help she gave to many of them. But Ezra was unmoved, and continued his tirade. "Ye may take the witch-wife back," he said, with a roughness that was partly genuine and partly assumed to help him overcome some secret, lingering weakness. "Let her lie in some of the black places in the woods where she would foregather with her master the Devil; but her wicked body shall never poison the ground where Christian folk are buried. No grave in consecrated ground for the likes of her."

The exchange continued in the shadow of the meetinghouse, and with everyone taking a side and voicing their opinion, Parson Eaton could barely be heard. Goody Cole and some of the other women recalled how Hannah would sit by the bedsides of sick women whom no one would visit, as well as how she visited a woman who had a terrible ordeal after the birth of her child. These women broke from the crowd and ran up to the coffin, bowing down on their knees in prayer.

Even still, there was no man of Harpswell who stepped forward to carry the coffin of Hannah Stover into the burial ground. In the end, the fishermen's wives who had carried it down the shadowed road, lowly singing hymns, were the only ones who made sure that Hannah received a proper burial. They carried Hannah's coffin to her final resting place in the burial ground behind the meetinghouse.

The final exchange that day between Johnston and Parson Eaton offered no peace between the two parties.

"Ye have buried a witch," Johnston muttered under his breath as they left the sacred spot.

"We have made the grave of a saint," Eaton replied solemnly.

ORR'S ISLAND CEMETERY

The attention, care and respect the small coastal cemetery on Orr's Island receives is evident in an initial glance. The recently cleaned white marble stones shine brilliantly on a sunny day. Broken and cracked stones have been repaired and reset onto their bases. The grounds and landscaping are welcoming to the casual visitor, who can stop and read the stones going back to when the cemetery was established in 1838. While the community of Orr's Island is contained in just one thousand acres, the cemetery itself is small, at just under five acres. Before the cemetery was established, the dead were buried on Harpswell Neck, and people had to travel by boat for church services and funerals. William and Frances Orr donated the first parcel of land that had soil deep enough to dig the graves in.

Here you will find the graves of people who truly lived a long and productive life near the salty seaside air. There was Ellen Hanson, who died at the age of 104 in 1968. Born in Lisbon, Maine, in 1864, she ran a dry goods store and dairy business with her husband, Lewis, on Orr's Island. At the age of 99, she spearheaded a campaign to raise $150 to shingle the roof on the Freewill Baptist Church, of which she was the oldest member at the time.

Another gravestone speaks of longevity:

> *William Gilliam*
> *Apr 4 1902*
> *AE 102y 2m*
> *A light is from our household gone.*
> *A voice we loved is stilled.*
> *A place made vacant in our home.*
> *Can never more be filled.*

A very unusual gravestone can be found for Little Benny Chase, who was one year and ten months old when he died on August 10, 1856. A shield with a small circular window surrounded by tiny flower buds and two doves drinking out of a chalice in the design offers symbolism that speaks of innocence and a life cut short. The extremely rare window frame suggests that a small cameo photograph would have been set into the stone, but it is unfortunately now lost to time.

The gravestone for Little Benny has a tiny window frame that would have held a small photo.

The carving of a sleeved hand, complete with buttons at the wrist, grasps a cross on the gravestone for Ephraim Johnson, who died at the age of thirty-three on April 5, 1882. A delicate carving of lily of the valley flowers adorns the gravestone for Mary Ann Littlejohn, who died on April 30, 1881, at the age of twenty-four. The lily of the valley is a flower of the spring and represents the promise of the spirit being renewed and a return to happiness.

Active fundraising efforts are being put forth by the cemetery committee to build memorial monuments to veterans who are both full-time and summer residents of Orr's Island. Continued maintenance and upkeep are also long-term plans endeavored by this committee of one hundred people, which represents a surprising 15 percent of the population of the island. This small island town leads the way in making sure that those who walked and fished these shores—whether 180 years ago or 5—will be remembered and that their gravestones will continue to tell their stories.

MIDCOAST MAINE

ROCKLAND ALMSHOUSE BURIAL GROUND

Hidden away at the edge of the woods on an unassuming private road called Squiggle Hollow Lane in Rockland, Maine, is the Almshouse Burial Ground. The only small plaque marking the cemetery is being overtaken by a quickly growing pair of juniper bushes.

Almshouse were a regular part of Maine communities in the nineteenth century. Towns would find ways to help support people who could not help themselves or did not have families to support them. In Rockland, these people were known as "inmates" of the almshouse. These "inmates" included children, the homeless, unemployed people, the disabled, people with mental issues and single mothers.

Sometimes public appeals would be made within certain groups to keep people out of the almshouse. In the *Dental Independent* in 1890, the following request was published:

> *A Dentist, 95 years old, in Rockland, Maine is in extreme poverty. To prevent his being taken to the almshouse, T.E. Tibbetts of that town asks remittances to give him support for the few remaining days he has to stay on earth. Bretheren, send a few dollars to Dr. Tibbetts for this poor man. Dr. Wm McDavis, President of the State Dental Society, says it's a particularly worthy cause.*

The sign for the Rockland Almshouse burial ground is partially hidden in the bushes at the edge of the cemetery.

There were others who reached out to those living in the Rockland Almshouse, such as the Christian Temperance Union of Maine. This group referenced the facility in its annual report:

> *Rockland has an especially comfortable home for the poor. Almshouses are visited and cheered by our White Ribboners; in some song and prayer are held; almost without exception the inmates are remembered with gifts. Children are still found in the almshouse. Many have been taken from there to other homes. When greater preventative means are taken to shield children from neglect, and to assure to them the proper training in good citizenship, there will be fewer paupers and fewer criminals in our state.*

The almshouse itself was described in 1913 in the First Annual Report of the State Board of Charities and Corrections:

> *Net cost of maintaining the almshouse last year—$2160. Salary of Superintendent—$360. Building is of wood, 3 floors, 18 rooms, 13 of*

them sleeping rooms. Largest number of beds in a room 2, average 1. Building has modern toilets, sewage connection, city water supply. Sexes are separated all of the time except at meals. Present at the almshouse November 1, 1913, 7 males, 7 females. Four of the inmates are between 2 and 16 years of age.

On May 9, 1994, a proposal was put forth before the City of Rockland to mark the burial ground, which had almost completely disappeared. Research at the time revealed that ownership of the land dated back to the early 1700s, when it was owned by Earl Tolman, one of the area's earliest settlers. The poor farm was built in 1830, and the inmates were described as people who were sickly, as well as veterans who had been forgotten. In 1959, the almshouse was shut down due to a fire, after which all the land, with the exception of the burial ground, was sold off by the city. The hope in marking the grounds was that future generations would not lose track of those who were buried there.

The grave markers on the property in 1994 were described as being riddled with bullet holes, accompanied by tattered flags. There was even a silver marker that read "Unknown sailors 1942"—likely in reference to the six dead German sailors who were taken to the cemetery from the wreckage of a U-boat that sank near Mount Desert Island. That marker is currently missing from the grounds. Only a few marked graves remain:

J David Lantz

"Unknown Name" 1967

John W Smith 1889–1965

Walter Leroy Dudley 1889–1941

The bronze memorial plaque placed in 1994 on a rock is hidden quite well at the edge of the burial ground, but if you push aside the vegetation, it reads:

Rockland Almshouse Burying Ground

In remembrance of those who lie buried here.

Over the years, the sick, the indigent and those whose families were unable to provide for their care, spent their last days at the City Almshouse that stood near this site. Their names have been lost to history, but they are not forgotten.

By order of the Rockland City Council In the Year of our Lord, Nineteen Hundred and Ninety Four. Thomas J. Molloy, Mayor.

FOREST HILL CEMETERY, SPRUCE HEAD

Within the Forest Hill Cemetery in Spruce Head, Maine, is the inspirational tale and unique grave for a brave female lighthouse keeper whose story continues to evoke a dramatic chapter in the state's maritime history. Maine is currently home to sixty-five lighthouses, which dot the coast to guide and guard its thriving waterways. At one time, lighthouse keepers were appointed by U.S. presidents, as their jobs were so vital in making sure that the lighthouses stayed operational. In the case of Abbie Burgess, she took on the job of lighthouse keeper unexpectedly at a very young age.

In January 1856, Abbie was just seventeen years old, and she lived with her family twenty-five miles offshore on the island of Matinicus Rock. Abbie's father, Samuel Burgess, was the keeper of the lighthouse on the island, known for being a challenging station to work at. Waves would wash over the keeper's house and the tops of the twin lighthouses that stood guard during heavy storms. It was not uncommon for windows to be broken after storms and boulders moved across the island. A storm was raging on the island while Abbie's father was away getting supplies in Rockland, and it was left up to her to tend to her family's needs, including those of her ill mother.

The roiling waters of the Atlantic Ocean soon covered the island, and since it was up to Abbie to keep the family safe, she moved them all into one of the

The grave for heroic Abbie Burgess can be found in a small cemetery in Spruce Head.

An aluminum lighthouse was placed on Abbie's grave by historian and author Edward Rowe Snow.

lighthouse towers. Meanwhile, Abbie continued to climb the stairs to the towers with supplies to make sure that the light stayed lit during the storm. The move was a wise one, as the keeper's house was soon washed off the island into the sea. The challenge of keeping the family fed was another that Abbie had to contend with, but she managed to save the family's chickens, keeping them in the tower during the ordeal. Abbie did her best to keep a brave countenance as she rationed cornmeal to the family each day for nearly four weeks, until it was safe enough for her father to return to the island. Tales of Abbie's ordeal and heroics made her a household name throughout the coast of Maine.

In the following years, Abbie married the son of the next lighthouse keeper at Matinicus Rock, Isaac Grant. They had four children together, and Abbie became the assistant keeper at Matinicus Rock. In 1875, the couple continued their service at Whitehead Lighthouse. Abbie was fifty-three when she died in 1892, but before her death, she wrote that if she were going to have a gravestone, she wanted it in the shape of a lighthouse or a beacon. In 1945, Edward Rowe Snow—historian, author and "Flying Santa" to New England's lighthouses—granted Abbie's wish. A gathering at Abbie's grave revealed a small aluminum lighthouse placed securely over her grave.

The story of Abbie Burgess inspired several books chronicling her life and experience during the fateful storm of 1856, including a popular book called *Keep the Lights Burning, Abbie* by Peter and Connie Roop. In 1997, the Coast Guard commissioned the "Keeper Class" *Abbie Burgess*, a 175-foot buoy tender, to provide service to the coast of New England. The work of the buoy tender includes search-and-rescue, security and domestic ice-breaking assignments. The tender is stationed in Rockland Harbor and is responsible for covering the area from Boothbay Harbor to the Canadian border.

Abbie's work is done, and her story, much like the symbol of the lighthouse on her grave, guides people to visit and leave inspirational tokens behind, honoring her bravery in the face of adversity.

MacPhail Cemetery, Owl's Head

Some cemeteries keep their secrets hidden so well that their stories all but disappear except for a nondescript scrap of mysterious stone situated among more carefully carved and remembered markers. That is the case with the strange concrete slab of stone with no distinctive carvings located at the MacPhail Cemetery in Owl's Head, Maine. One thing is for certain: this story is a reminder to not overlook any random blank stone in a graveyard.

In 2019, Walter Guptill—a member of the Maine Old Cemetery Association, volunteer and cemetery enthusiast—stumbled on a strange slab on concrete that seemed to be more than meets the eye. Upon further investigation, he discovered that the stone recalled a 1911 tragedy that was all but lost to the newspaper archives. Published in the Rockland, Maine *Courier-Gazette* on Saturday, September 2, 1911, was the following article:

> *A quadruple funeral, requiring three hearses, was the strange spectacle which Main Street beheld Wednesday afternoon—the aftermath of the Bennett tragedy at Ingraham Hill, which so greatly shocked the whole country last Monday. Rev. Russell Woodman, rector of St. Peters church who appears to have been Edward Bennett's sole confidant, arrived home Tuesday and immediately took charge of the funeral arrangements, which he insisted should have the utmost privacy as being the undoubted wish of the unfortunate man. Admitted to the Burpee undertaking rooms where the simple rites were held, were less than a dozen persons, who had been associated with the deceased through his daily occupation at the Littlehale grain mill in this city.*
>
> *For the gathering Rev. Mr. Woodman read the special psalm and lesson appointed by the Episcopal church for suicides. For the murdered children, Edward, Barbara and Nancy, there was a short office. The casket occupied by the father was in the center of the apartment while grouped near its head were the three tiny white caskets containing the innocent and beloved children who in the brightness of life's beginning had been sacrificed by an abnormal and disordered mind. There were no relatives to shed tears over the remains, but two compassionate neighbors and friends had sent floral tributes and the casket of Edward Bennett was not neglected. The pall-bearers were Edgar A. Burpee, John Brazier, Louis Smith and Frank George. As the procession moved southward through Main Street there were many spectators, and many words of sympathy and sorrow were spoken. The bodies of Nancy and Barbara were placed in one hearse, while the father and son each occupied another. The burial at the Ingraham Hill cemetery, in four graves alongside Mrs. Bennett's, consisted of a brief service.*

Mr. Bennett apparently was so grief-stricken over the recent loss of his wife that he couldn't handle it—he murdered his children with chloroform

An irregular, nondescript stone slab covers the grave of the Bennett family in Owl's Head.

and then drowned himself in the ocean. In an interview with Reverend Woodman, he stated, "He had never seen such absolute agony as when Mr. Bennett knelt by his wife's grave and lifted his eyes skyward without sound or word. It was indeed the grief that does not speak, whispers the o'er-fraught heart and bids it break."

The article continued with a quote from Owen Wister, who was a contemporary American writer at the time: "Somewhere in every grown man is a boy who is afraid of the dark." Trying to help the reader comprehend what had happened in Mr. Bennett's mind, the article described the former state of the dead Englishman as "alone in a strange land with a hopeless future from his standpoint."

Walter Guptill, who brought this story to recent attention, researched library and probate records in regards to any further details about the burial site. He discovered that a gravestone had been purchased. The gravestone, now missing, is believed to perhaps be underneath the concrete slab, out of view. The undeniable grief of Mr. Bennett and the sadness surrounding this tragic event is forever silenced underneath a bare, emotionless stone.

BELFAST

The robust and vibrant city of Belfast offers visitors much to explore and discover, whether stepping into the shadow of maritime history along the waterfront docks, taking a ride along the preserved historic railroad line or walking the inviting rail trail. Stately homes perched on the hills of the city tell stories of industry and success. The final resting places for some of the earliest residents of the city blend into the growth and development that happened in the nineteenth century.

It is said that the name Belfast was settled on after a coin toss, and in 1773, the town became officially incorporated. One of the first cemeteries in town can be found off Searsport Avenue, called the East Belfast Cemetery. Some of the people buried there can be counted among the first settlers who came up from Londonderry, New Hampshire. The wooded area consists of gravestones carved out of slate and marble. One particularly interesting gravestone with a winged skull is for Ruth Brown; the carving reads:

> *In Memory of Ruth Brown*
> *Wife of John Brown Junr.*

Departed this Live
April 1st, 1798
Aged 30 years & 3 Mo.
Also her infant incircled
In her right arm
Aged 4 Days

Another burial ground was established on the west side of town, and the first documented burial took place there in 1790. With the establishment of Grove Cemetery in 1830 on Belmont Avenue, burials continued there, and the grounds were expanded over the following years. The remains from the west side burial ground were supposed to have been moved to the Grove Cemetery as the neighborhood was redeveloped. However, despite the graveyard being moved, there were more than traces of it remaining underneath the houses, as discovered numerous times in the early twentieth century.

An excerpt from the *Bangor Daily News* of September 12, 1908, reads:

While excavating for a cellar and drainage on the place recently bought of Clarence Wyman by Capt. George Fletcher, the workmen came across several boxes which proved to be old coffins containing the remains of bodies buried many years ago. In what was known as the old burying ground, situated just below High Street. Many years ago the bodies, as many as were marked were taken up and removed to the Grove cemetery and the land occupied by the burying ground was made up into house lots. The bodies lately exhumed were doubtless overlooked at the time. They were found to be laid about four feet deep and in what looked to be plain, sawed cedar boxes. The boxes were well preserved so that the side boards could be lifted out. On one lower jar which was found the teeth were almost perfect and some of them very white. Some of the skulls looked very much like Indians, but of course it is impossible to tell who or what they are. The local authorities were notified and ordered the bones buried.

In July 1912, the old burial ground made another appearance, much to the dismay of a local city resident; the *Bangor Daily News* shared the details of the story:

Mrs. Sarah Nealey has complained to the city government that this frequent digging up of skeletons, skulls, ribs and miscellaneous anatomical exhibits on her premises is getting on her nerves. She says that it is very annoying to find vertebrae of departed Belfast folks strewn about the place. She would like to have something done about it.

Some months ago a sugar barrel filled with bones was exhumed from the land on which Mrs. Nealey's house stands. These were taken care of by the city and buried in Grove cemetery. A short time ago, while digging to lay a pipe, a black walnut coffin was exhumed in such an excellent state of preservation that it took three hard knocks with a pickaxe to break it open. It could not be learned, there being no marks of identification, whose remains had been thus rudely disturbed.

The matter was discussed at the Saturday night meeting and the City solicitor stated that at the time the old cemetery which occupied the land, now bounded by High, Union, Pearl and Spring streets, forming a square, the city gave a quit claim deed to the property and agreed to remove all the bodies. This was done so far as marked graves went but during the past 50 years, since this was done, skeletons have now and then been brought to light. The matter was therefore referred to the committee on cemeteries, which will investigate the matter further and report at a special meeting.

It is said that the old cemetery was the first to be established on the west side of the river or in the city proper is situated, there having been an earlier one on the east side.

After Grove cemetery, the present place of burial in Belfast, was laid out, many of the ashes and bones of those laid at rest in the old cemetery were removed to it by surviving relatives. In 1847, it is said that the old cemetery had fallen into such a state of decay and dilapidation that the town was indicted for neglect. Cattle roamed at will over the graves and several buildings were erected within the limits of the yard. Some time about 1850 an action was taken to remove all the remaining bodies to Grove cemetery and a quit claim deed of the property was given to private parties.

According to Williamson's history, many graves were not discovered at that time and excavations between High and Union streets have often brought to light the bones of the departed. As of late November, 1874, in excavating near the northerly corner of Union and Pearl streets, three graves remained. A coffin plate was exhumed, bearing the inscription "James Gilbreth, aged 30" with the Masonic square and compass. Mr. Gilbreth was a millwright who lived at the Head of the Tide, and was buried with Masonic honors in 1820.

The city officials feel that if the city looks after the bones which are accidently exhumed that it is doing all that can be expected and this has been done whenever there has been occasion. "We do not intend to institute

An angel holds an ornate harp over the grave of Philo Chase.

a search and seizure for dead bodies," said Mayor Hanson this morning, "but having done all that we can, the matter will be further investigated by the cemetery committee."

It was business as usual at the Grove Cemetery, and it became the final resting place for politicians, governors, military heroes and residents of the area. The cemetery is quite extensive today, and there's a tremendous number of Victorian-era markers to be found, along with museum-worthy statuary. Upon entering through the main gate of the cemetery, one cannot help but notice the larger-than-life angel sculpture on the grave for Dr. John Brooks. Originally from York, Maine, he graduated from Dartmouth College and earned his medical degree from Jefferson Medical College in Philadelphia. He came to Belfast in May 1851 and practiced medicine for about thirty years, until ill health caused him to retire. A successful businessman with many business connections and interests, he became a senator and later mayor of Belfast by an almost unanimous vote. Considered a wealth of information and a prominent citizen, according to his obituary, the turnout at funeral service at a home on Church Street was quite large.

Left: A life-size angel can be found overseeing the Brooks family plot.

Right: The small grave for Mildred Stover reflects a variety of Victorian symbolism.

Next to the Brooks angel is another large angel sculpture for Philo Chase, who died at the age of sixty-eight on November 5, 1898. Oddly, in 1857, he married Mary Elizabeth, who later went on to marry Dr. John Brooks in 1899; she died in 1911 and is interred in the doctor's plot.

The lichens have been recently cleaned off the delicate gravestone for Mildred H. Stover, who was just over ten years old when she died in 1897. The images carved on the stone include an unrolled scroll—symbolizing a life span with the past and future hidden from view. There is also a broken harp—to symbolize a life cut short—as well as a variety of realistic-looking carved marble flowers.

A polished granite stone can be found for Percy Sanborn, and on it is carved the word *Artist*. Percy died at the age of eighty in 1929. He was a self-taught artist who was born in Waldo, lived most of his life in Belfast and specialized in painting ships and cats. His work can be found in many notable museums and collections, including the Penobscot Maritime Museum and in the marine collection of the Mystic Seaport Museum. Some of his early paintings he sold for just five dollars, but now collectors purchase them for tens of thousands of dollars. Percy was even known to paint theater backdrops. A man of a keen eye, who captured the history of the age of sail in his paintings, summed up in a simple word: *artist*.

The Grove Cemetery is a wonderful place to visit if you enjoy getting lost among acres of tombstones and memorials to those who passed through and lived in Belfast. Take a closer look at the carvings and inscriptions to see the many different ways those sleeping forever underneath them are remembered.

Union Cemetery, Southport

Take Dogfish Road to the Union Cemetery in Southport and you'll discover a white marble lighthouse grave marker that resembles nearby Hendricks Head Lighthouse at the entrance to the Sheepscot River. The man buried near the marker is Captain Jaruel Marr, who was appointed as the head lighthouse keeper at Hendricks Head as compensation for the wounds he suffered serving in the Civil War. Jaruel, along with other men from Southport, walked sixty miles to Portland, Maine, to enlist in the Seventh Maine, Company D, of the Union army, and he left a wife and three young children behind. Jaruel ended up being wounded in the war and was incarcerated in the Confederate army's Liberty Prison in Richmond, Virginia. A Union doctor named Wolcott nursed him back to health, and eventually Jaruel named his son after the man who helped him.

Jaruel was very devoted to his job as lighthouse keeper at Hendricks Head, as evidenced by a review of the keeper's logs that he wrote. During a severe coastal storm, he recorded in his journal that the winds and waves moved a huge boulder, eight by twelve feet, twenty-one feet from its original resting place. Jaruel Marr and his wife, Catherine, had five children, and all three of their sons became Maine lighthouse keepers. Two sons, Clarence and Preston, became keepers at Pemaquid Point Light and Portland Breakwater Light, respectively. Their son Wolcott Marr entered the lighthouse service in 1890 and first served as an assistant at the Cape Elizabeth Two Lights and then at the Cuckolds Fog Signal Station. His next station was his childhood home.

On July 1, 1895, Wolcott Marr wrote of the retirement of his father in the log at Hendricks Head: "Arrived at this station at 2:00 p.m. to relieve Mr. Jaruel Marr, who has been keeper here for the past 29 years." Jaruel died on March 13, 1907, at the age of seventy-seven; his wife followed in 1920. A separate double gravestone for Jaruel and Catharine displays an oak tree with acorns at the center of the stone, symbolizing longevity, strength and endurance.

The Union Cemetery is also the final resting place for the mysterious "Lady of the Dusk," whose apparition can be found walking along Hendricks Head Beach in Southport according to legend. The mysterious woman, who arrived by bus on December 1, 1931, and registered at the local hotel as Louise G. Meade, wanted to see the open ocean. Witnesses described that she was wearing dark black and set out on the long walk by foot. A woman named Mrs. Pinkham, who worked at the post office in Southport, recalled seeing her and the conversation that they had together. While Mrs. Pinkham was concerned about it getting dark and cold out, the mystery woman was not deterred in any way and continued about her walk. After that conversation, no one saw the woman again, and she did not return to the hotel.

Toward the end of that week, the locals became quite concerned about the woman's whereabouts, and they formed a search party. A group searching the beach near Hendricks Head Lighthouse made the startling discovery. The woman's body was caught in the undertow, bobbing up and down in the tide. When she was pulled out of the water, it was believed that she had committed suicide, as an iron was found tied to her hands and a leather belt was wrapped around her wrists. Newspapers far and wide carried the story in the hopes of identifying the mystery woman, but even with the help of New York City detectives, no information was discovered.

The Union Cemetery did not have a potter's field, and the townsfolk gave the woman what was called a decent funeral; by all accounts, she was buried underneath a tree off to one side of the cemetery. For a time, simple stones were piled in the spot, but they have all but disappeared. The area where she lies has become almost as much of a mystery as the woman herself. To this day, some people tell the story of a ghostly figure seen wearing a long black dress walking the road to the fateful beach at sunset.

OWL'S HEAD LIGHTHOUSE, OWL'S HEAD

Sometimes animals can be just as hardworking companions as their masters, and one faithful springer spaniel named Spot is buried at the bottom of the staircase to Owl's Head Lighthouse at the entrance to Rockland Harbor.

Right: Owl's Head Lighthouse stands on a high, rocky outcropping at the edge of Rockland Harbor.

Below: The grave for Spot, the lighthouse dog, can be found at the bottom of the walkway to the lighthouse.

The keeper of this important lighthouse from 1930 to 1945 was Augustus Hamor, and his daughters, Pauline and Millie, taught Spot how to pull on the rope to ring the fog bell. Spot had a way of communicating with the passing maritime traffic, he would ring the bell as the vessel approached, and they would respond with the sound of a horn or bell. Stuart Ames, who captained the local mail boat, became one of Spot's most anticipated visitors, as he always made sure to have treats to share with him. Spot became so good at recognizing Captain Ames that he could tell the sound of his engine as it drew near.

One day, a blinding snowstorm blew into the harbor, and because of blowing winds, the bell could not be heard as the captain approached the dangerous rocky ledges. Spot found his way to the shore as the storm raged, and he started barking loudly and continued to bark until he heard the sound of the mail boat whistle response. Lucky for the captain, he was able to figure out his position and proceed safely around Owl's Head.

After Spot's passing, a gravestone, carved with "Spot, the Lighthouse Dog," was placed on his final resting place. Many people actually stop and pay their respects to Spot before they climb the long staircase to the lighthouse. There is also the lingering ghost story about Spot still being on the job. The legend is that when a storm has moved in along the coast, you can sometimes still hear Spot barking to help guide and guard those navigating around the large promontory of land.

THOMASTON VILLAGE CEMETERY

With more than six thousand graves, the Thomaston Village Cemetery is full of compelling stories and oft-visited graves, as some sections are still being used for interments. The Elm Grove Cemetery can be found just next door, with about five hundred burials. A large sign points in the direction of one of the most visited graves on the grounds, for Henry Knox. His story is summarized on the sign as follows:

Former bookseller, Henry Knox, became a respected military strategist, artillery expert, and friend of George Washington, serving with him in most campaigns during the Revolutionary War. He is best known for hauling 60 tons of canon from Fort Ticonderoga, NY to Dorchester Heights, MA in the winter of 1776 to drive the British troops out of Boston Harbor. When the

British withdrew their last troops from New York on November 21, 1783,
Knox headed the American forces that took over. He stood by Washington
during his farewell address on December 4th, and became the senior officer
of the army. Knox went on to serve as Secretary of War, first under the
Articles of Confederation, and then in Washington's cabinet.

In 1795, Knox retired to Montpelier, the estate he built in Thomaston on land inherited by his wife, Lucy Flucker Knox. General Knox died suddenly in 1806. The graves of Henry Knox, Lucy and their family were moved to Village Cemetery when Montpelier was demolished in 1870 to make way for the Knox and Lincoln Railway. There are many interesting facts surrounding the life of Knox after the American Revolution ended. When he retired to Thomaston, he invested in several business ventures, including businesses in the timber industries as well as agriculture and lime quarries. Unfortunately, none of his ventures made him any significant money, and he amassed quite a bit of debt.

The grave for General Knox was moved from his property to grounds that he established for the town of Thomaston.

Knox's death came after he swallowed a chicken bone that resulted in an infection that took his life over the agonizing span of a few days. His funeral was described as having an imposing procession, preceded by a company of militia marching with arms reversed. A company of artillery, followed by a company of cavalry, preceded the coffin. The general's hat and sword rested on the coffin. His favorite horse followed behind, with the boots of the late rider reversed in the stirrups. A long procession of family, friends and mourners followed the spectacle. Knox was buried underneath his favorite oak tree, but because the tree roots and ground continually shifted during spring thaws, his tomb was moved twice on his property. The cemetery that Knox lies in today is land he actually donated to be used by the town for burials of the dead. A replica of General Knox's mansion was rebuilt on its original site in 1929 and can be visited today.

Within a short walk from the grave of General Knox is a gravestone with a beautifully carved ship. The stone reads:

Capt. Geo Jordan
Born Feb. 22, 1813
And sailed from Liverpool
on the Unfortunate Pacific
Jan. 23, 1856

Captain Jordan had sailed to England and had booked return passage on the steamship *Pacific*. The steamer first launched in 1851 and had set a new transatlantic speed record in its first year of service. When the steamer left Liverpool, there were about two hundred passengers and crew on board; within a matter of days, the ship disappeared. Five years after the *Pacific* went missing, a message in a bottle was recovered on the remote island of Uist, off the west coast of Scotland, that explained the fate of the ship. The story was chronicled in the *New York Times* on August 7, 1861:

The copy of the contents of a slip of paper, found in a bottle some weeks ago, on the western coast of Uist, in the Hebrides, and forwarded to us by our agent at Sternoway. The paper in question, apparently the leaf of a pocketbook, used in the hurry of the moment, was covered on both sides with pencil marks, from which the following was with difficulty deciphered:

On board the Pacific, from L'pool to N. York. Ship going down. [Great] confusion on board. Icebergs around us on every side. I

Above: The original Montpelier was built in 1795 as a retirement estate for Major General Henry Knox and his family; after it was torn down, a replica home was built in 1929.

Left: A beautiful ship is carved onto the memorial stone for George Jordan.

know I cannot escape. I write the cause of our loss, that friends may not live in suspense. The finder of this will please get it published,

WM. GRAHAM.

If we are right in our conjecture, the ship here named is the Pacific, *one of the Collins line of steamers, which vessel left Liverpool on Jan. 23, 1856, three days before the* Persia, *and has not since been heard of; and this slip of paper, three inches by two, is probably the only record of the fate of that missing ship.*

The writer was evidently some person accustomed to the perils of the sea, for it is difficult to understand how any person whose nerves had not been hardened by the presence of frequent and appalling dangers, could have written with such manifest coolness in the immediate presence of death.

When this bottle was thrown overboard from the Pacific, *that vessel was surrounded by mountains of ice. This tiny receptacle of the only record of a magnificent ship, escaped the crash which obliterated all traces of the vessel from which it was thrown, was carried, in all probability, thousands of miles on the ice, and was only released when the ice melted in the tropical sun. Thence, the presumption is not a violent one—this fragile messenger was swept by the Gulf Stream, and carried along the course nearly to the extreme verge to which, as we are told, the Gulf Stream is propagated. This bottle was found on the Western shore of the Hebrides, where it arrived under the mysterious guidance of those influences which have of late years so earnestly engrossed the attention of scientific geographers.*

The ship was declared sunk by icebergs, and the story almost was lost to history; however, in 1991, wreckage was located in the Irish Sea off the coast of Wales and was believed by many to be the *Pacific*. The epitaph on the stone for Captain Jordan reads:

Frail is the tenor of our mortal breath
Yea in the midst of life we are in death.

SEAVIEW CEMETERY ROCKLAND

The Seaview Cemetery in Rockport, Maine, seems to be the perfect place to take a walk on a sunny morning; however, you may feel a chill at the edge of the cemetery approaching a particularly sad gravestone. The gravestone reads:

> *Unknown*
> *Unwanted*
> *Baby Boy*
> *Found in*
> *Rockport Quarry*
> *April 20, 1940*
> *Age About 5 Months*

Surrounding the gravestone are toys and mementos left by compassionate visitors. A heartbreaking discovery was made on April 21, 1940, when a passerby noticed a body floating in an abandoned and flooded lime quarry

Toys, gifts and token of remembrance can be found surrounding the gravestone for the "Quarry Baby."

A large boulder surrounded by smaller stones can be found for Dr. Benjamin Spock.

near the town line of Rockport. The body was determined to be that of a baby boy between the ages of four and five months old. An autopsy revealed that the child was deceased before he was thrown into the quarry. Public appeals were made looking for any information about the child and his parents. After an exhaustive investigation, it was determined that the case could not be solved. Members of the community raised enough funds to commission a grave marker for the child's burial.

In June 1995, Ted Churchill, living in Rockport, Maine, died when the car he was driving hit a tree in Lincolnville. He was a filmmaker and teacher who had expressed wanting to be buried next to the unknown baby boy. Ted was a regular visitor to the gravestone, and according to reports, he felt a bond to him. However, his request was denied by the town.

Also buried at the Seaview Cemetery is noted doctor Benjamin Spock, who died at the age of ninety-four in 1998. Dr. Spock was an accomplished and admired pediatrician, and he was the author of the bestselling book *The Common Sense Book of Baby and Child Care*, which was first published in 1946. He was a vocal advocate for children and civil rights. Dozens of beach stones are piled around his grave marker, some with sentiments written on them.

STRANGER GRAVE, GRAY, MAINE

Located at the crossroads in the center of Gray, Maine, is the Gray Village Cemetery, which has been in use since the 1780s. Confederate flags and American flags wave side by side on a most curious grave found along one

A Confederate flag flies over the grave of the "Stranger" in Gray.

of the long pathways. A perplexing story about this Civil War soldier has persisted ever since the grave was opened to lay this "Stranger" to rest. The little town of Gray sent proportionally more sons to the Civil War than any other town in Maine. Within the Gray Village Cemetery, there are buried more than 178 Union soldiers. The Stranger's story, scarred by tears of tragedy and triumph, began with the death of Lieutenant Charles H. Colley, the twenty-nine-year-old son of Amos and Sarah Colley of Gray. When the war began, Colley joined the Federal forces and was placed in Company B of the Tenth Maine Volunteers.

Gray, a town of about 1,500 people, had sent nearly 200 of its native sons to battle. Charles Colley was mortally wounded at the Battlefield of Cedar Mountain, Virginia, and died at the Alexandria Hospital in Virginia. His body was sent home for burial. However, when the casket was opened, it revealed the body of an unknown soldier in a gray Confederate uniform. It seems that the army had put his casket on the wrong train. As they were unable to correct the mistake, and believing that the young man's family would want him to have a proper burial, the soldier was laid to rest in the town cemetery. In theory, the townspeople of Gray could have sent the body of the Stranger away, but they did not.

About a week later, a second coffin containing the remains of Lieutenant Charles Colley arrived, and he was buried in the Colley family plot, not far from the Stranger's. When the war ended, money was collected by the Women's Relief Corps of the Grand Army, and they were able to obtain a gravestone for the unknown Confederate soldier. For many years, the Daughters of the Confederacy, a women's heritage association, sent a Confederate flag, also known as the Stars and Bars, to be placed on the grave. In fact, there were many people who were moved by the story and sent flags as well.

In the May 30, 1977 edition of the *Bangor Daily News*, Dorothy Heseltine, curator of the Gray Historical Society (which is next to the cemetery), was interviewed about the mysterious Stranger. Dorothy said, "There are theories that both were killed at the same time or that their names may have been similar. I feel it is a touching story. This person missing all these years and his family never knowing what happened."

The identity of the Stranger remains a mystery to the townspeople to this day, and he is buried just one hundred feet from Lieutenant Charles Colley—their stories forever intertwined. There is a bit of irony in the fact that an unidentified Confederate soldier dressed in gray has his final resting place in Gray, Maine.

PINELAND CEMETERY/ MALAGA CEMETERY—NEW GLOUCESTER

There are some people who believe that if certain chapters of history are lost, we will never learn from them. The story of Pineland Cemetery in

New Gloucester brings back the stories of people who were marginalized and treated poorly. Exploring this cemetery and remembering those who are buried here is just one step toward giving the dignity back to the people who deserved it.

Some of the people buried here were disinterred from the burial ground on Malaga Island, and others are those who died at the nearby school for the "feeble-minded." This gruesome chapter in history is reflected in the cold uniformity of the evenly spaced grave markers. There is not so much as an epitaph or an angel on these very simple stones, as if they weren't worth memorializing, but theirs is a story worth telling.

Pineland was a state facility that opened in 1908 as the Maine School for the Feeble-Minded at the Pineland Center in 1996. Due to the horrific conditions and abusive treatment of residents, Pineland was placed in federal receivership in 1976 and finally closed in 1996. Institutions like Pineland "treated" people with developmental and other disabilities by segregating, hiding and even sterilizing children and adults, without their consent and based solely on their disability. There were many who died at the facility, and their bodies were never claimed, so they were buried in the Pineland Cemetery. There are dozens of stones here marking the existence of forgotten souls. It is quite amazing to walk around the burial ground and find many who had died under the age of twenty. In the early years, the graves were simply marked by a cylinder of cement with a number on top. At its peak in the mid-twentieth century, there were 1,500 residents and 240 employees at Pineland. In the 1950s, proper burial markers were placed in the cemetery, listing names and ages when research could find them.

A few miles up the road, Pineland has been completely refurbished, and there are no signs of what used to be a dreary facility for many. Today, Pineland is a five-thousand-acre working farm, with a variety of businesses housed in the former buildings on the property. An array of recreational events take place on the rural property. The memories of those who passed through the doors, willingly or unwillingly, reside just down the road now in a peaceful burial ground.

There are also seventeen graves in this burial ground that mark another disturbing tale of forgotten Mainers. Malaga Island, just off the coast of Phippsburg, was a small community of hardworking people. Some of the jobs of the people on Malaga included fishing, lobstering, clamming and carpentry. The wives would stay home and take care of their children while the fathers worked. They built little shacks for houses and used skiffs to get around on the water. With complete autonomy, separate from Maine towns, the island was referred to by some as "No Man's Land." It became such a hard way of life for some on the island that many sought support from the mainland.

Those who shunned the islanders called Malaga an "eyesore" and a "maroon society." In addition, the people of the island were a mixed race of Irish, Scottish, Portuguese and African American, and some of them were runaway slaves. Mixed-race marriages were common on the island and not a popular notion on the mainland at that time. The *Casco Bay Breeze* and other newspapers nosed around in the 1890s and printed stories about a "degenerate colony," where indiscretions included the use of tobacco and tea, adding to the negative opinions held by the mainlanders. A schoolhouse was built on the island, and the children of the island were taught to read and write. An article in *Harper's Magazine* from 1909 described the people of the island:

> *The ocean creeps to the doors of their huts and the winter waves thunder in their ears—and there are those who say that the din of the sea beats curious ideas into the head.*

None of the neighboring towns wanted to support Malaga with the funds or supplies that they needed, and Phippsburg actually denied aid to the island and gave the island up as a "ward of the state." On July 14, 1911, Governor Plaisted and his council visited Malaga. The governor deemed the conditions deplorable and recommended burning down the shacks. On August 5, 1911, the plan was to give the people on Malaga two weeks to get off the island, and the governor declared that the "Malaganians must move."

People on Malaga Island were paid for their homes, which were swiftly destroyed upon their exit from the island. Even the burial ground on the island was uprooted, and eighteen bodies were reburied in five large caskets in the Pineland burial ground. All of the nine headstones reflect the year 1912, the year that they were reinterred here. One stone marks the grave of five children; another marks the grave of three.

Unfortunately, some of those who were evicted from the island ended up being committed to the School for the Feeble-Minded. While a few families were taken in by families on the mainland, others died within a few years of leaving the island. For many others, it was difficult for them to fit in with the mainland communities.

Calls for a formal investigation into how this injustice happened to the community of Malaga were initiated in 2001. The Maine legislature in 2010 did issue an apology at the start of its spring session. In July 2017, a new memorial in the cemetery was unveiled. In attendance during the ceremony were descendants of the Malaga community. Governor Paul LePage spoke at the ceremony and was instrumental in providing a source of state funding for the memorial. In addition, a scholarship was also established for Malaga descendants. The importance of establishing a memorial was expressed by the attendees as a reminder of compassion and humanity that was long overdue to the people of Malaga.

The granite memorial bears the names of those forced by the state to leave their island homes and a summary of the history:

> *From the 1860s until 1912, a community of laborers and fishermen lived on Malaga Island. Off the coast of Phippsburg A controversial community for its time White and black residents married and lived together on the small island until the state of Maine evicted them in 1912 Included in the eviction was the state's removal of the island cemetery to the grounds of the Maine School for the Feeble Minded, where some island residents were committed Remembered here are the community members exhumed from the Malaga island cemetery by the state and those who died here as patients*

It is still a matter that is tended to by many who want to be a voice for the injustice and indignity for marginalized communities of Pineland and Malaga. Those who care to visit the burial ground find it a tremendously sad chapter in the history of Maine, nearly forgotten and lost forever.

FRENCH CEMETERY, LINCOLNVILLE

Almost hidden and set back from Route 1 in Lincolnville is the French Cemetery, which is one of the oldest burial grounds in town. The first "official" burial took place in 1815, for Olive Rogers; however, fieldstone markers indicate that the burial ground was first used in the 1700s. There are many sailors' graves and at least twenty-three war veterans buried on the grounds dating back to the War of 1812. A group of volunteers still maintains the cemetery, and the views along the hillside are quite scenic.

It was a fateful trip to a scenic view that resulted in one of the graves being dug on the grounds in 1864. On the grave marker is carved a large *F* and the name French at the bottom. A small stone on the ground reads

Above: A large marker can be found for the French family at the French Cemetery in Lincolnville.

Right: The spelling of Elenora's individual marker is different from the spelling on the family marker.

"Elenora." It was May 7, 1864, when eleven-year-old Elenora French joined her sister, friends and a teacher and headed to the mountains in Camden. The group decided to climb to the top of Mount Megunticook (meaning "great swells of the sea" in the native language) to take in the beautiful views. They all safely reached the summit and were rewarded for their efforts by the breathtaking sights before them, but sadly the day would end in tragedy.

Elenora's sister recalled the story for the *Bangor Daily News* in a July 23, 1915 interview (as "Mrs. Frank Cassens"):

> *I remember exactly how she looked the last time I saw her. The wind was blowing very strongly that afternoon and her hat had blown off, taking with it her net. In those days the girls, little and big, wore their hair in handmade silk nets of various colors, not the hair-nets of today. When I last saw her she was sitting on a rock near the edge of the cliff, putting on her net. I turned away to speak to my companion. I heard a scream. I looked towards the spot where Elenora was sitting and it was vacant. I am 71 now, but if I live to be a thousand, I shall never forget the horror of that moment. She was gone, with that piercing scream. I think I must have gone insane for those first moments, although I am told that I did not faint. We all ran to the edge of the cliff but could not get near enough to look over.*

Elenora French plummeted more than three hundred feet to the rocks below. She fell at about 2:00 p.m., and it was sunset when her body was removed gently on a bed of pine boughs; she never regained consciousness and died just after midnight. Those who viewed her body were surprised to see what little damage had been done to her clothing and appearance. Dr. Estabrooks, the attending doctor, concluded that she died from her internal injuries.

Her sister said, "I have never been on the cliff since that day and for many years could not bear to even look at the mountains, but time softens all things, although it seems like yesterday when I recount the events of the day."

A white cross was erected at the site to honor her short life by inventor and millionaire Joseph B. Stearns, who built the stone mansion Norumbega in Camden. The steel cross has been replaced, vandalized and repaired several times, even once having the National Guard involved in hoisting it onto the mountain. Thick cables keep the cross secure today, marking the fateful spot.

In April 2011, a couple, Charles Black and Lisa Zahn, retired teachers from Kansas, had moved to the coastal community of Camden. But they argued over an online affair Charles had with an Arizona woman and how he spent some of Lisa's considerable inheritance money. They decided to take a hike up the trails to Maiden Cliff one afternoon.

Prosecutors said that an argument ensued and Charles hit his wife three times on the head with a rock before pushing her off the eight-hundred-foot Maiden Cliff. They both tumbled down the mountainside, and both were hospitalized for more than a week. Lisa said that she believed he was chasing her down the mountain, while Charles told investigators that he had no memory of hitting her or pushing her off the cliff. He told police that he had collected two rocks while they were on the mountaintop with the thinking that they'd toss them over the cliff, symbolizing getting rid of old baggage and hoping for a fresh start. Charles was found guilty and sentenced to ten years for attempted murder and aggravated assault.

The walk up the trail to Maiden Cliff is filled with oak and ash trees, which are much older than their stunted forms appear due to them growing on the rough mountain terrain. Tall, wiry grasses blow in the changeable winds, and many people believe that on occasion, the spirit of Elenora is present, preventing any other deadly accidents. Some stories tell of people who get close to the edge and hear someone shuffling behind them, and when they turn to look, there is no one there.

COLONEL JONATHAN BUCK, BUCKSPORT

Old legends never die—it just seems as though they dance on the grave in Bucksport, Maine. One of the most commonly told graveyard legends comes from this little old seaport town along the Penobscot River. Interred in a small family plot near the center of town along Route 1 is one Colonel Jonathan Buck. The plot is easily found, as a tall granite obelisk with a strange marking is found in the middle of the grave site. The inscription on the stone reads:

> *Col. Jonathan Buck*
> *The Founder of Bucksport A.D.*
> *1762*
> *Born in Haverhill, Mass*
> *1718.*
> *Died March 18, 1795*

On the other side of the monument is the single word *BUCK*.

Is the strange foot design on Johnathan Buck's grave the result of a witch's curse or something else?

The stone shows no carved images by the stonecutter. However, there is one ingrained image that appeared within months of the marker being erected back in 1795. It is clearly the outline of a foot, just above the Buck name. The stories behind this mysterious foot have brought the town a bit of notoriety, especially from those interested in old Maine legends.

Jonathan Buck wanted to build a shipyard near his hometown of Haverhill, Massachusetts, but the townsfolk weren't interested in his aspirations. He decided to head north and settle along the Penobscot River, and there he built a sawmill and a prosperous general store. He was named a colonel in Maine's Fifth Militia in 1776 during the American Revolution. In 1779, he served under Brigadier General Solomon Lovell to defend the important waterways of the Penobscot.

A difficult siege ensued, with the British driving the American defense fleets up river to Bangor, where they were eventually defeated. About 150 sailors and soldiers were killed, and another 300 were wounded or missing. The fleet was abandoned and was subsequently burned by the British. Johnathan Buck escaped with his wife, Lydia, and youngest daughter to Brewer. He then walked from Brewer all the way back to Haverhill and remained there until after the war ended in 1783. He then returned to the settlement, which was now called Buck's Town. He died twelve years after his return, and the town was then renamed Bucksport.

A monument to Buck was erected by his descendants sixty years after his death, and after a few decades of weathering, the foot and a witchcraft story appeared. The tall tale was read in newspapers across the United States in the winter of 1899. The story described Colonel Buck as a believer in Puritan ideologies; he was strict and uncompromising, but most of all, he would not suffer a witch to live in his community. The story went that an old woman, who was an outsider in the community, was accused of witchcraft, and she soon faced trial for her misdeeds and for being in league with evil incarnate. She was ordered to be imprisoned and persuaded to confess her crimes; she refused the pressure but was found guilty and sentenced to be hanged.

The details of the legend explained that the gallows was located on a rocky hill across from the cemetery in town. As she was escorted to the gallows, she allegedly cursed the judge for ordering her death and pleaded for her life. Colonel Buck made a motion to hasten the woman to the gallows. The hangman prepared the old woman for her execution, and it is said that in her last moments on earth, she uttered the legendary curse:

Jonathan Buck, listen to these words, the last my tongue shall utter. It is the spirit of the only true and living God which bids me speak them to you. You will soon die. Over your grave they will erect a stone, that all may know where the bones of the mighty Jonathan Buck are crumbling to dust. But listen! Listen all ye people—tell it to your children and your children's children—upon that stone will appear the imprint of my foot, and for all time long, long after your accursed race has perished from the earth, the people will come far and near and the unborn generations will say, "There lies the man who murdered a woman." Remember well, Jonathan Buck, remember well!

The story went on to explain that the hangman carried out his duty, and the infamous curse hung in the air over an astonished crowd.

Curious people traveled to see the unusual formation on the stone that looked like the outline of a leg that some supernatural draftsman sketched on the granite. It was rumored that numerous attempts were made to remove what some considered a "stain." The theory that the witch was dancing on the grave was captured in a story published in 1902 *New England Magazine* story by J.O. Whittemore.

The legend seemed to overshadow the explanation that there was an imperfection in the stone that caused lichens to grow in the outline of a leg. In a 1949 interview with the *Portland Press Herald*, Mrs. Esther Terrill of the Bucksport Library stated that people from as far west as California would write to her concerning the execution of a witch. Her response to the inquiries explained that there was no evidence to verify the legend.

There are still descendants of Colonel Buck living in the area of Bucksport today. Hundreds of people pass by the gravestone every day, and a few of those curious folks stop and look at the stone and contemplate the legendary curse that is almost as old as the town itself.

DOWNEAST AND ACADIA

ATUSVILLE CEMETERY, MACHIAS

It's difficult to count all the lost settlements and abandoned small villages in Maine. However, sometimes when it seems as though the memory of these places will be gone forever, a reminder from the past reaches out to us like a distant voice in a dark forest at night. The voice of this burial ground can be heard softly along Court Street in Machias, Maine. In the center of a small clearing is a stone monument that was placed in 2005 to mark the lost African American settlement and burial ground of Atusville. The marker reads:

> On this lot are a burial ground, and the remains of a school, which once served as Atusville in the African-American community, from the late eighteenth century to the mid-twentieth century.

There is no list of names and no grave markers on this hallowed ground. The sun streams in through the trees, sending long beams of light through the shadows across the area surrounding the single stone.

It was in April 1980 that the Maine Old Cemetery Association stepped forward as the Town of Machias was considering moving forward with plans to turn the site into a gravel pit for the town's landfill. MOCA referred to the 1841 deed, which noted that the four-acre property was sold to the town for fifty dollars to remain a burial ground and to be used for no other purpose. The story of the site emerged from the shadows to reveal a chapter in local history that few people were aware of.

The American Revolution saw the service of former enslaved Africans and two men, London Atus and Richard Earle, who had come to Machias to build a community. Slavery was abolished in New England in 1784, and these two proud veterans were very hopeful to build a life under a newly formed nation. The community grew as it connected with both white families and Native American households. In 1795, a woman from Atusville was the target of a riot in response to her filing a paternity suit against a well-respected white man. The ideals of this small settlement continued to be challenged as the nineteenth century progressed. In what had been set up as a burial ground for the families was soon turned into a schoolyard for the Atusville children by 1853. The children had been bullied and harassed in the local school by some of the white children, so a school was specifically built to serve them without any intrusive threats to them or their education.

The burial ground reportedly didn't ever have proper markers, rather the people were buried in mounds with the possibility of some wooden markers that are long gone. The population of the village dwindled in the twentieth century, and the last person living there died in 1965; nothing remains of the schoolhouse. According to University of Maine college professor and author Marcus LiBrizzi, the grounds are haunted. He described unusual photographs taken on site that display strange shapes and anomalies. Could it be the reflected light of the sun showing in these mysterious photos, or is it the light of the past shining out of the darkness as a reminder of what many have forgotten?

BROOKSVILLE BURIAL GROUNDS AND CEMETERIES

First explored as early as 1605 and located on Penobscot Bay, the town of Brooksville is located along scenic shores and coves. The area was once called Maijorbigwaduce and also Plantation Number Three. Officially incorporated in 1817, the town was named for Massachusetts governor John Brooks, who was an officer of the militia who led his troops in the Battles of Lexington and Concord and served under George Washington in 1776.

In the mid-seventeenth century, there were several altercations between the Native Americans and the white men of the area. After these incidents, the Native Americans would seek refuge in the area now known as Walker Pond in Brooksville. In the spring of 1660, a fishing vessel at Punch Bowl Cove in Eggemoggin Reach was captured by the natives, the crew was killed and the boat was burned.

Under the command of a local church, men who were seeking revenge for the attack came up with a plan. They landed in an area that is now known as South Brooksville and captured a Native American. They promised not to kill him if he would lead them to the village retreat near the pond. The group arrived at the village as the sun rose. It was the height of the summer and what was known as "green corn season." The Native Americans were sleeping, with no one posted to guard the village, having had a celebratory feast the night before. The men in the party killed everyone in the village except for one brave, who escaped.

Ancient human bones have been unearthed in the area of the pond, indicating an Indian burial ground. Also discovered were stone arrowheads, spearheads and other implements. The soil near Walker Pond is still reported to have traces of charcoal mixed in it from the seventeenth-century fire.

There are many small and family burial grounds in Brooksville, with as few as two people buried in a location. Some are only accessible by crossing private property, and others are hidden in the woods under broad fern fronds, while still others are along the shoreline and have been lost to memory.

West Brooksville Congregational Church can be found on Route 176, Coastal Road. This single-story wooden church was built in 1855, and a well-kept cemetery can be found adjacent to the church behind a white fence. Recent efforts to clean and maintain the sixty or so gravestones that remain is evident. Some broken stones can be found at the edge of the cemetery, and small, modern markers can be found replacing the stones on a few of the graves, lest the memory of those interred here be lost. Some gravestones speak clearly of their stories through carefully carved letters. A white marble stone with a cracked base tells the following story:

> *Jennie Alma Died Apr. 9, 1863, AE. 5 ys. 8 ms.*
> *Annie Atkins Died Apr. 6, 1871 AE. 3 d's.*
> *Kind Stranger pause and weep,*
> *for we were very beautiful,*
> *but sickness came and we had to die,*
> *and have gone to play with the angels.*
> *Children of Isaiah & Ruth Lord.*

A small square carving in the stone seems to offer a possible frame for a portrait or decorate carved ornament:

> *Mrs. Julia*
> *Wife of Daniel Carter*
> *Died Oct. 1, 1859, AE 23 yrs.*
> *Was it my heavenly Father's will*
> *to call her home so soon!*
> *Then I will love that Father still*
> *and her beyond the tomb.*

A broken rose and two broken flower buds are carved within a marble circle, symbolizing three lives cut short. The stone reads:

> *Mrs. Sarah,*
> *wife of Capt. J.N. Lord,*
> *AE 22 yrs. & her infant son*
> *& daughter.*
> *Died April 26, 1862.*
> *Gone like a faded flower,*
> *no more on earth to bloom;*
> *Redeemed by Christ's redeeming power,*
> *they live beyond the tomb.*

Lanes Island Burial Grounds and Cemetery

Standing in between the patches of high grass, looking along the rugged shores amid sparkling indigo waters, feeling the ocean breeze all around you—Lanes Island in Vinalhaven is the ideal place to spend forever. The island remains a place of eternal rest for some, although that may not be the main attraction for many. Owned by the Nature Conservancy, the forty-five-acre island offers beautiful coastal trails to explore. There is much to be discovered, connecting visitors to the people who have walked this island hundreds of years ago, if one knows where to look.

A small family cemetery for the Lane family can be found on the island. The tall white marble obelisk tells part of the story. The front is inscribed:

Capt. Timothy Lane
Died June 12, 1871
Aged 66 y's, 5 m's, 12d's
Rebecca C. his wife
Died Feb. 3, 1888
Aged 81 y's, 4 m's, 5 d's

Along another side is inscribed:

Charles A.
died Sept. 3, 1849
AE 4 y's & 8 m's

Margaret S.
died Dec. 28, 1837
AE 11 m's & 23 d's

Children of Timothy and Rebecca C. Lane

Captain Timothy Lane found success at sea as he quickly moved through the ranks from mate to master. Eventually, he owned nearly twenty trading and fishing vessels, with the largest being a 119-ton schooner that was built in Boston in 1864 named *Rebecca C. Lane*. In 1857, he built his ten-bedroom Greek Revival home on the island. The house, built by experienced shipbuilders, overlooks Carver's Harbor. It had been abandoned for a time but has since been restored and can be visited in a short walk from the cemetery.

The success of Captain Lane wasn't just measured in the fleet of ships that he owned but also in the business that he started with his brother, salting codfish and shipping it all along the East Coast as far away as the Caribbean. By the time Captain Lane passed away at the age of sixty-six in 1871, he had established a life centered on the island that still bears his name. He left behind a wife and four children.

Also in the cemetery is the grave of Timothy's father, Benjamin Lane, who was born in Gloucester, Massachusetts, and moved to the area after the American Revolution. Benjamin purchased the land that was originally called Griffin's Island (and later Lanes Island) from Thaddeus Carver for price of two cows.

A gravestone can be found in the cemetery for Margaret S. Lane, Timothy's daughter, who died at eleven months old in 1837. There are also gravestones for the Roberts family members, as Thaddeus married into the Lane family in 1818.

The most curious gravestone is still a bit of a mystery, and while it appears to mark a grave, there is no one buried beneath it. The cracked stone is for Doris Armstrong, who was born in 1932 and died in 1991. The stone was discovered on the clam flats near the beach around 1992. In trying to solve the mystery, it was determined that there was a record of a "family of Doris Armstrong in Belfast" visiting the island. It was supposed that perhaps the family had come to the island to spread Doris's ashes and left a memorial stone. Two area residents who tried to solve the mystery decided that it would be best to have the stone placed in the Lanes Island cemetery instead of leaving it precariously in the clam flats.

In 1847, according to the records of the Maine State Historical Society, Lanes Island was at one time a burial ground for the Native Americans. According to an article penned by Edward Russell:

> *There is no spot, to my knowledge, which has ever been called the Indian planting ground, but there is little doubt, that Lane's Island was their burying place—that island from the nature of the soil would be most likely to invite their attention. As the banks of the island cave away, human bones have been exposed to view for many years. A skeleton which I examined myself, five years ago, was buried with the head to the south and the feet to the other, and not more than twelve inches below the surface of the ground.*

A newspaper report in May 1939 told of the death of Gust Carlson, a fifty-eight-year-old stonecutter who suffered a heart attack in a pit on Lanes Island trying to exhume the "skeletons of three Indians." A boy who was digging for arrowheads made the initial discovery, and Dr. V.H. Shields, an amateur archaeologist, confirmed that the skeletons had been buried there for centuries. Some places in Maine can be small in size and sometimes unassuming at first glance, but when you look closely, you can find the unexpected stories of legendary people just below your feet.

Pine Grove Cemetery, Cherryfield

Decoration Day was established three years after the Civil War ended by General John A. Logan. General Logan was part of an organization of northern Civil War veterans who was seeking a nationwide day of remembrance for those who had died in battle. He declared the following: "The 30th of May, 1868, is designated for the purpose of strewing with flowers, or otherwise decorating the graves of comrades who died in defense of their country during the late rebellion, and whose bodies now lie in almost every city, village and hamlet churchyard in the land."

At the turn of the twentieth century, Decoration Day also became known as Memorial Day. In 1971, Memorial Day became an official federal holiday. In archives throughout America, there are stories and photographs of Decoration Day assemblies, parades and speeches. Stepping back in time to the Memorial Day of 1915 in Cherryfield, Maine, one can see how this was a day for the community to come together and remember those who gave their lives to defend this land and their beliefs.

The bell chimed at 2:00 p.m. at the Hiram Burnham Post, No. 50, headed by the Cherryfield Brass Band as it marched from the Grand Army of the Republic Hall to Union Hall. The hall was decorated with evergreens, flags and festoons of the national colors. There was prayer, shared by Reverend Clarence Fogg; a four-piece quartet that provided music; a reading of President Lincoln's Gettysburg Address; and a tribute to Betsy Ross. Afterward, the group assembled—some took to riding in cars, but the band marched, followed by two hundred schoolchildren carrying flags as the group headed to the Pine Grove Cemetery. The graves were decorated, a service was held at the soldiers' monument, the flag was saluted and "America" was sung by the gathering.

The group then proceeded to the town wharf for more readings, music and prayer. Twelve children carried baskets of flowers and threw them in the water in a custom of remembering sailors who had been lost at sea. The group returned to the banquet hall for a supper served by the Woman's Relief Corps.

Today, Cherryfield is the self-proclaimed "Blueberry Capital of the World" and is located along the Narraguagus River (which in the native Abenaki language means "above the boggy place"). The population is just about 1,300 residents but peaked around 1902 at around 1,800 people.

The beautiful arched gate for the Pine Grove Cemetery invites visitors in to explore the more than two thousand graves that can be found here. One of the grave markers that is quite a standout is a white marble monument for Union brigadier general Hiram Burnham (for whom GAR Post No. 50 is named), who was killed at the Battle of Fort Harrison in Richmond, Virginia. The carving on the stone reads "Died for the Union," and it features four flags, a large star and other ornamentation carved on it. The back of the stone reads:

Gen. Burnham
was killed in battle at
Chapin's Farm near
Richmond, Va.
Sept. 29, 1864
AE. 50 years

More than 4,000 Union soldiers were killed along with 1,750 Confederate soldiers in the Battle of Fort Harrison alone. The fort was renamed Fort Burnham after the general's death and still stands as an important historical Civil War site in Virginia today.

Beals Village Cemetery, Beals Island

"Tall Barney" was a Maine folk hero who many people believe was Downeast Maine's version of Paul Bunyan. He stood at six feet, seven inches tall and was a direct descendant of Manwarren Beal, the island's first settler, who first arrived in 1773. It was written that when Barney sat in a chair, his hands touched the floor. One day, Tall Barney was fishing off Black's Island; in objection to him being so close to English territory, sailors boarded his sloop, intent on capturing it at gunpoint. Barney took the guns from the sailors and allegedly broke them over his knee and threw them back into the British boat. A story from a Portland, Maine saloon recounted how he was harassed by fifteen men—he singlehandedly showed them their mistake in picking on someone bigger than them.

Many other legends persisted about Tall Barney—when he lay down in bed, his feet would stick out the window of the house. Allegedly, he drank water out of the hole of a 150-pound barrel, and he could easy lift cargo that weighed two hundred pounds out of the holding areas of ships. Alice Frost Lord, a columnist from the *Lewiston Evening Journal*, published a ballad written about Tall Barney in 1938; here is an excerpt:

Tall Barney Beal

A Barney Beal Ballad
When Maine could boast of giant pines
And brain and brawn in huge designs,
Manwaring Beal begot a son
No less than a phenomenon.
Mere five feet folk were puny lot,
And six feet people somewhat squat,
For Barney Beal was six feet plus,
With seven inches fabulous.

He new no fear and slight restraint,
When others frothed or made complain,
But settled every quarrel quick,
With energetic kick or lick.
His fingers touched the sanded floor
Whene'er he entered neighbor's door
And sat him down to chat a bit
And swear and boast and often spit.
'Tis said the women folks well knew
Their kitchen chairs would fall in two
Unless they tucked them out of sight
And left stout bench to take his height.
All up and down the coast of Maine He roved.
A human hurricane
They came to call Gunpowder Beal
And let alone from head to heel.

Barnabas Coffin "Tall" Barney Beal III died on February 1, 1899, at the age of sixty-three, some believe from heart strain. He had twelve children with his wife, Phebe, who is buried with him at the Beals Village Cemetery on Beals Island. The seven-foot monument to Barney towers over other markers on the grounds, and the epitaph states that he is "Peacefully Resting." The story of Tall Barney is looked on fondly by many, and at one time there was even a restaurant named after him in Jonesport called Tall Barneys.

Cutler Cemetery, Cutler

This story provides just one answer to the question, "What do you do with a person's body who died at sea?" While New Englanders have come up with some creative methods over the years, the story of Jeanette Blunt of Cutler, Maine, seems to be a local favorite. Jeanette married Captain Tristam Thurlow Corbett, who was the master of the ship *Lena Thurlow*. In 1873, Jeanette sailed with him to Matanzas, Cuba, which was part of the West Indies trade route.

Jeanette came down with a fever and died at the age of twenty-six while they were ported there. The captain decided to store and preserve her body in a cask of rum for the voyage back to Maine. When the ship returned to Maine, it was flying a pennant that signified that there was a death on board, and when the captain's wife wasn't seen on deck, it became obvious that she had died. When the burial service was arranged a few days later, it was decided that the rum barrel would also serve as her coffin. Jeanette's white marble gravestone can be found at the Cutler Cemetery in Cutler, Maine, relaying that she died in Matanzas on July 21, 1873. Her husband remarried a few years later and is buried in New York.

Union Cemetery, Southwest Harbor

Located in Southwest Harbor is the Union Cemetery, which can be found behind the Manset Union Church on Route 102A. Once known as the Manset Burying Ground, it is one of the oldest graveyards on Mount Desert Island. The stones here have shifted quite a bit over the years, and some are very difficult to see and read. It was recorded that the earliest markers here were simple fieldstones.

The 1938 book *Traditions and Records of Southwest Harbor and Somesville* by Mrs. Seth S. Thornton described some of the gravestones and stories that could be found there:

> *In this yard the grave of Nicholas Tucker is marked by a stone inscribed "Died in a foreign land July 14, 1839, aged 63. What is your life? It is of a vapour that appeareth for a little time and then vanisheth away." It is said that Mr. Tucker, when he shipped his last voyage, took with him materials for his coffin as he said he had a presentiment that he would never*

return. A son, Andrew Tucker, who died April 22, 1819, at the age of two years and a daughter Amanda M., whose death occurred in 1833 at the age of three years lie nearby, also a grandson, Horace D. Tucker, who died in 1860 at the age of one year. This stone is skillfully carved with the figure of an angel bearing a child in her arms.

This burial ground like all others has many graves of young mothers and little children. We read the record of "Cordelia, daughter of Joshua and Lavonia Mayo, died 1850, aged 15." This little girl was said to have amused herself during a thunder shower by holding her head under the dripping eaves of the house, from which proceeding the child took cold and died. Mothers in this vicinity ever since have told this story to their children and warned them against such experience.

The cemetery is also the final resting place for Jonathan Brown, who served with John Paul Jones in 1780 on his flagship and took part in several famous naval battles. There are many graves for multiple children who died in the 1850s due to the diphtheria epidemic that swept through the community.

HILLSIDE CEMETERY, HULLS COVE, MAINE

In 1688, King Louis XIV of France granted a piece of land to Antoine de la Motte Cadillac that later became known as Mount Desert Island. Cadillac went on to become governor of Louisiana and a commandant of Detroit and MacKinaw (Michigan), and he would sign his correspondence "Lord of Donaquee [also known as Union River] and Mount Desert in Maine." Eventually, Cadillac returned to France and died there. Cadillac Mountain in Acadia National Park was named for the intrepid French explorer.

In 1786, Cadillac's granddaughter Madame Marie Therese de Gregoire came to Maine to stake their claim to the property. With a stamp of approval by Thomas Jefferson and the French ambassador the Marquis de Lafayette, sixty thousand acres of land—or about 60 percent—of the original grant were awarded in a Massachusetts General Court.

A mystery remains as to what happened to the couple's fortunes over the years. Their property was sold off piece by piece so that they could live modestly. Speculation about the majority of the fortune included the theory that it was buried somewhere on the island, or perhaps some went to France, where their three children were living. There are no records as to the details, and the children never claimed the property in Maine. In the end, the two were left destitute, though beloved by the hardworking locals.

When Bartholemy de Gregoire died in 1808, it was reported to be a cold winter day, with high snowdrifts that piled up all over town. The snow was so deep that it was impossible to enter the graveyard, so a grave was dug just outside of the churchyard walls and he was laid to rest there. Madame de Gregoire left the family home and moved in with the family of Captain Samuel Hull, dying two years later at the age of sixty-five. A boulder marks the grave for Madame de Gregoire, and the answer to the whereabouts of the family's fortune lies with her.

VILLAGE BURYING GROUND, BAR HARBOR

The Village Burying Ground is located in the heart of bustling downtown Bar Harbor and can be found situated between the Bar Harbor Congregational church and St. Saviour's Episcopal Church. An interesting historical note is that the parish hall for St. Saviour's church was used as a navy barracks during both world wars.

Upon entering the burial ground, a sign greets you that reads:

> *Established before 1790 holds in many unmarked and unknown graves the remains of those courageous men and women pioneers on the frontier of downeast Maine. Sea captains, fishermen and farmers, shipwrights and hotelmen, selectmen and legislators, their wives and children, and the occasional sailor dying far from home also rest here. Strong commitment to the Union is remembered by the monument dedicated in 1897 by the Town of Eden already world-renowned under the later name of Bar Harbor.*

There are many wonderful examples of Victorian gravestones to be found on the grounds. Many have been cleaned and repaired in recent years. A beautifully carved hand holding a bouquet of flowers is seen on the gravestone of Zella Cook, who died on January 22, 1885, at the age of twenty. A sleeping lamb is found on the gravestone for Addie Florence Higgins, who lived a short sixth months and fourteen days, dying on May 24, 1871. The symbolism of the lamb represents purity and innocence.

Israel Higgins Jr. was an accomplished mariner over his career and was the captain of the ship *Hazard* out of Little Cranberry Island and the schooner

The memorial marker for Captain James Hamor depicts a ship in a stormy sea.

Julia Ann out of Bar Harbor. He was forty-five years old when he was lost at sea. His marble gravestone bears a lot of ornate symbolism, including clasped hands, an hourglass with large feathery wings and a wreath with rosettes on it. Part of the inscription on it reads:

Erected by Capt. R.G. and S. Higgins.
In memory of Capt. Israel Higgins who was lost at sea
March 23, 1823. AEt 45 yrs.
Also his wife Polly Higgins who died Feb. 26 1818 AEt 36 yrs.

A large urn tops the monument for Captain James Hamor, who died at the age of seventy-nine on December 17, 1873; a detailed carving of a ship being taken over by a wave is carved on one panel. Captain Hamor's wife, Clarissa, is buried beside him; having died in 1888 at the age of eighty-five. The sentiment carved on the stone reads:

He'll ride no more the billows
Nor o'er the rolling wave
He has performed life's final voyage
And anchored in the grave.

While the population of Bar Harbor swells in the summer and people find themselves exploring the natural beauty or visiting the many shops and restaurants in the town, a visit with the former residents of the community in this cemetery is highly recommended.

THE MAINE HIGHLANDS AND AROOSTOOK COUNTY

Mount Hope Cemetery, Bangor

Modeled after Mount Auburn Cemetery in Cambridge, Massachusetts, as a garden-style cemetery, the Mount Hope Cemetery in Bangor has some of the most beautiful Victorian-era memorials in the state of Maine. The cemetery was much needed by the community, as older burial sites had become filled, and with the growth and development of Bangor, some of those older burial grounds were being unearthed. There are about thirty thousand people interred here in over 264 acres of land.

There are many stories about the surprising discoveries of burials being unearthed around the city of Bangor, which makes interment at Mount Hope much more appealing to those who wish to remain undisturbed. In the 1830s, a road construction crew reportedly dumped human remains with the soil on a worksite. The secret was revealed when a coffin was seen sticking out of the ground. In 1977, a site being prepared for a pumpkin patch on Essex Street behind the Naval Reserve Center revealed a tombstone for a four-month-old girl named Elizabeth Bruce, who died on May 13, 1819. While the stone mentioned that she was the daughter of William and Susan Bruce, there was very little information that was found. There was a Bruce homestead off Valley Avenue in Bangor, but it could not be determined for certain if she was a member of that family. In addition, it could not be verified if her remains were still on the Essex Street site where her gravestone was found, or if she had been moved to Mount Hope in later years.

The first burial that took place at Mount Hope was for Samuel Call, who died at the age of fifty-eight on July 9, 1836. However, there are older gravestones that can be found at Mount Hope with interesting backstories, such as the 1791 slate gravestone for Joseph Junin. Joseph was originally interred in a cemetery on Hammond Street, but those who were buried there were later moved to Mount Hope. Joseph was a storekeeper, and many historians refer to him as the first murder victim in Bangor. The story went that Joseph was murdered by his nephew, who falsely blamed the crime on local Native Americans. Since there was no evidence to substantiate his story, he was arrested and tried for his uncle's murder and found guilty. In a strange twist, he received a new trial in which he was acquitted. The nephew inherited his uncle's estate and promptly moved to France.

Near the State Street entrance of the cemetery is a section for the children who died while living at the Bangor Children's Home. The stones there span the second half of the nineteenth century. There are two lots for Civil War veterans, as one lot at the front of the cemetery filled so quickly that another lot was established for fallen soldiers.

An ornate Greek Revival monument can be found on the grave of nineteenth-century industrialist and lumber baron General Samuel Veazie, who died at the age of eighty on March 3, 1868. General Veazie was a shrewd businessman and founded a town he named after himself, which was a lumbering community between Orono and Bangor. The establishment of

In the early 1930s, the Webber Waiting Room was commissioned for visitors awaiting the trolley.

this namesake town was voted on in 1853, with the reasoning that the taxes being paid by the citizens were too high, as they were supporting services and needs in downtown Bangor.

An empty space can be found between the grave of John Thomas (who died in 1878) and a small grave with a dove on the top. The little grave reads "Our Baby" on the front, with a lily flower. That unmarked grave is believed to be the final resting place for Fanny "Fan" Jones, born in 1830 as Nancy W. Jones in West Brooksville, Maine.

When Fanny arrived in Bangor as a young woman, she took up the profession of prostitution. She was described as a fashionable woman, and by the 1850s, she was operating a successful brothel. She was known as the madam of the Sky Blue House of Pleasure on Harlow Street in Bangor. Harlow Street was in the heart of the city's red-light district, which was sometimes referred to as the "Devil's Half Acre." It was said that the chimney of the house was tall enough to be seen from both the water and the woods and was a perfect landmark to attract customers. Despite a few minor setbacks, Fanny ran a thriving business, offering an average of eight working women, who were more seasoned than the girls found at the other brothels in town.

It was reported than once a year Fanny purchased Parisian gowns for her ladies, and she would travel with them in an open coach to the Bangor State Fair. The women would then set up a tent at the fair where they could socialize and meet potential customers. In the 1860s, Fanny met an ex-con named John Thomas, who moved into the brothel with her. She may have officially married Thomas, but the assumption was she became his common-law wife. The brothel was spared from the Bangor Fire of 1911; however, just six years later, Fanny died from tuberculosis at the age of eighty-one. Fanny had purchased her Mount Hope burial plot during the Civil War, and the small gravestone that reads "Our Baby" is thought to be the child of Fanny and John.

One song archived at the University of Maine Folklore Center at Orono captures a logger's love of Bangor's Sky Blue madam:

> *Fan Jones, she ran a cathouse*
> *Way down on Harlow Street*
> *If you're a woodsman*
> *Head straight there*
> *And your friends you'll surely meet.*

Left: The Skofield Memorial is similar to the Tholos Temple at Delphi, Greece.

Right: The ornate urns at the entrance to the Webber family plot have heavenly details on all sides.

The Skofield memorial at Mount Hope is a granite ring supported by eight ten-foot pillars and is similar to the Tholos Temple at Delphi, Greece. Inside the circle is carved:

> *Erected to the Sacred Memory of a Gentle and Loving Mother by Her Devoted Sons MCMXXVII.*

The granite that was used to build the memorial was quarried in Barre, Vermont. The large, polished granite marker on the ground reads:

> *Amanda M. Harris*
> *Wife of*
> *Charles E. Skofield*
> *February 9, 1837*
> *September 8, 1920*

Amanda was born in Weston, Maine, and she had three children by her first husband, Thomas Gilpatrick, who died in 1864. Charles Ellis Skofield

Left: A sweet-faced angel is covering a tiny coffin on the grave for Channing Webber.

Right: This hillside staircase that leads to several graves was featured in Stephen King's film *Pet Sematary*.

was Amanda's second husband, by whom she had ten children, two of whom died as toddlers. The family lived on a farm in Hodgdon, Maine, and Amanda's son chose Mount Auburn for her as he thought it was the most beautiful place. Five of Amanda's children, along with their spouses and children, are buried in a circle surrounding the memorial.

Two beautifully carved urns bearing heavenly motifs can be found at the entrance to the Webber family plot. John Prescott Webber was originally from New Portland, Maine, and owned a successful lumber business and several general store. He had six children over the course of three marriages and died at the age of seventy-eight in 1911. At this plot is the grave for Anne S. Webber, who died on August 17, 1869. The inscription on the front of the stone reads:

> *More fondly we loved her,*
> *Than language can tell,*
> *Stern death hath removed her,*
> *But, yet all is well.*

The sentiment is continued on the back of the stone:

Tis sweet to die when gone before
The lov'd one of my heart—
My angel son says mother, come
We never more shall part.

A finely carved white marble angel sculpture, draping a cloth over a tiny coffin, can also be found in the Webber plot for little Channing, who was the son of John and Caroline (his second wife). Channing died the same day he was born, on November 13, 1881. The sculpture is quite remarkable; note the tiny details of the blanket fringe and toes on the angel.

There are so many fascinating graves and stories at Mount Hope that even a full day's visit isn't enough to see them all. Hannibal Hamlin, vice president to Abraham Lincoln, is buried here; he died in 1891 while playing cards in a city club. Impressionist painter Waldo Pierce was laid to rest here in 1970; some of his European-inspired paintings can be found in galleries around the world, including the Metropolitan Museum of Art. Infamous gangster Al Brady is also buried at Mount Hope; he was shot and killed by FBI agents in 1937 in downtown Bangor. Many people also come to the cemetery as fans of Steven King to visit the shooting location for scenes in the movie *Pet Sematary*.

CAMP ETNA CEMETERY, ETNA

Camp Etna, a Spiritualist camp that was originally established in 1848, is the final resting place for the ashes of one of the most accomplished (and at times controversial) Spiritualists of her day. The name Mary S. Vanderbilt and the year 1919 are carved on a lichen-covered boulder, with no additional inscription or epitaph. Mary's friendship was described as a gift by many, and her mediumship abilities were said to be second to none. Mary was born in 1867 and was originally from West Mansfield, Massachusetts. Her mother died when she was three years old, and she was raised by her aunt. Mary claimed that her first psychic vision came when she was fifteen years old.

The spirit of a Native American girl named "Bright Eyes" allegedly guided Mary's spirit communication for thirty-four years. Mary became known for her accuracy at private séances, and whenever questioned by skeptics, she seemed to have passed their inquiries and tests. As her popularity grew, Mary was even invited by the czar of Russia for a visit, and she toured throughout Europe giving readings.

Mary married George Pepper in the 1880s; he initially supported her work, but they eventually divorced. She ended up marrying lumber magnate Edward Ward Vanderbilt in June 1907. Edward's first wife was interested in the Spiritualist movement and the work that Mary was doing. After Edward's wife died, Mary claimed to have continued to communicate with her over the following years, which helped to ease his grief. The marriage of Edward and Mary was not without controversy, as his children from his first marriage tried to have him declared mentally incompetent in court based on his beliefs. Initially, he was deemed unstable; however, the decision was appealed, and the marriage was declared valid, which entitled Mary to the considerable fortune he had.

While there were detractors claiming that Mary was a fraud, her work continued at Camp Etna, with her speaking engagements sometimes attracting crowds of five thousand people. She served the camp for seventeen years, ten years of which she was the organization's president. Mary died after a brief illness on April 27, 1919, in Boston. Her last words to the public were, "I have found Spiritualism a good thing to live by, and I have come pretty close to finding it a good thing to die by."

Hundreds of tributes poured in after her death from grateful people who spanned all walks of life. Her sister, Harriet Scannel, wrote that Mary

The ashes for Spiritualist medium Mary Vanderbilt reside underneath this large boulder at Camp Etna.

was divinely gifted and that "she needs no epitaphs. The spiritual truth she taught, the great universal soul she was, the help she gave in loving service to humanity—these are her monuments."

A memorial book was published in 1921 called *Mary S. Vanderbilt: A Twentieth Century Seer*, written by by M.E. Cadwallader. The foreword of the book including the following passage:

> *In the great struggle between light and darkness, Mary S. Vanderbilt stood as a lighthouse, guiding souls to that harbor of truth, where they might find the glorious knowledge that their loved ones, who seemingly had died still lived and loved, and she, like all great souls, laid all upon the altar of truth.*

Earl Whitcomb Carter wrote the following poem for Mary just three days after her death:

> *Oh spirit rare! Who guided us so long,*
> *Along the rough and stony paths of life,*
> *Who hushed our fears,*
> *and taught us right from wrong,*
> *Who dried our tears, and helped us bear our strife.*
> *Speak to us now, and tell us it is best*
> *That thou shouldst leave us, whom we love so much.*
> *Help us to bridge the space that lies between,*
> *And give us strength and faith to feel thy touch.*
> *Thou who hast never failed, we miss thee so,*
> *Lend now thy hand to help us bear the blow.*
> *Speak out thy message ever clear, that we May still,*
> *from thee, God's wondrous wisdom know.*

It was a cold and quiet winter day when I stood at Mary's grave at Camp Etna, and my feet sunk into layers of snow and softened mud. I stood there and contemplated the amazing existence and influence of Mary's life to her followers who believed in life after death. It seemed fitting for me to pay my respects out loud; as I said goodbye, a large chestnut fell loudly with a *thud* from the tree that shaded Mary's grave, and I smiled.

Dixmont Corner Cemetery, Dixmont

Dixmont, Maine, is a small, rural town nestled in the hills. Originally called Collegetown in the late 1700s, the site obtained its name as part of a grant from the State of Massachusetts to the trustees of Bowdoin College. Dr. Elijah Dix of Boston purchased the township, and it soon became known on Dixmont. He was born in Watertown, Massachusetts, and practiced apothecary medicine in Worcester.

You can find a 1768 book called the *Formulary of Elijah Dix* in the Colonial North America Library at Harvard University. This handwritten book, which also refers to his studies with Dr. William Greenleaf, includes recipes for powerful elixirs, herbal ointments and powders using ingredients such as opium and camphor.

In 1771, a sensation rippled through Worcester when a man named William Linsey, who had been executed in 1770 for burglary, reappeared— or at least his skeleton did! Dr. Dix was in possession of William's skeleton and had been using it for the purpose of studying anatomy. According to reports, when it was discovered, a near riot broke out at his Worcester home. In response to the outraged community, the doctor took out an advertisement in the *Boston Gazette and Country Journal* on February 18, 1771, explaining the reasons for his actions:

> *To the Impartial Publick*
>
> *It is with great reluctance I appear in print, but it is become necessary as I have been represented to the Publick in an odious light, by a set of men who cannot bear any should live but themselves.*
>
> *To set this affair in a clear light, it is proper to acquaint the Publick; that about twelve months ago I set up an Apothecary Shop in Worcester, which was disagreeable to a certain number of men who would if possible monopolize (to themselves) all the Profits of the Town.*
>
> *In this situation my conduct was narrowly inspected and unfortunately for me I gave them an opportunity, by taking the body of one Linsey, who was executed on the 25th of October last, with no other view than the advantage of having a skeleton in town, whereby other surgeons, and myself, might gain further knowledge of the human structure.*
>
> *At this they rejoiced, proclaiming I had done for myself. I must leave this town, I out to be hanged & till they enraged some people to such a degree, that a number, after consulting lawyers to know if I had laid myself open*

The original gravestone for Elijah Dix now lies on the ground at his grave in Dixmont.

to the law (resolving to prosecute me without mercy), finding I had not, they came in a riotous manner to my house demanding the body, which I deliver'd; desiring they would keep it cover'd, as it was not in a condition to be seen; instead of taking my advice (with a view to irritate the minds of the people), they exposed it the remainder of the day to as many as they could collect, which had the desired effect, so much that they surrounded my house soon after, in the night, blowing horns, ringing bells, hanging up a dead dog before my door.

Not withstanding all they did, the thinking part of the people considering my ultimate design was to get knowledge, which I would tend to the Publick good, my practice and custom return'd as formerly. But being hitherto baffled in their attempts, they published an anonymous advertisement respecting me, as useing the body in an inhuman manner, and contrary to his desire (it was only known to a few) till after the affair happened.

And that their advertisement might take the greatest effect, they inform you that it is truth and attested by five respectable gentlemen: these gentlemen I allow to be as worthy any, and I believe the Publick will think so; when they are inform'd, they were requested to sign their advertisement, but one and all refused, on account of its being a spiteful, ill-natured malicious thing.

Having represented the facts, just truly as they were, I leave it to the impartial Publick; whether or not I ought to be represented to the world in such an infamous manner, as those men and their dependants have done.

After examining the whole with candor, I hope my friends and customers will see through their evil design, and continue their favours as usual.

I remain the Publick's most obedient humble Servant,

ELIJAH DIX

By 1795, Dr. Dix was living in Boston and operating an apothecary store in Faneuil Hall. Dr. Dix would visit the town of Dixmont on a regular basis and make long trips from Boston. Finally, in 1809, he became ill and died during one of those visits and was buried at the Dixmont Corner Cemetery. A single urn can be found on his white marble gravestone that reads:

> *In memory of Doctr. Elijah Dix*
> *of* BOSTON
> *who deceased in this Town*
> *of which he was the founder*
> *May 28, 1809*
> *Aged 62*
> *A man distinguished*
> *by strength of mind,*
> *active industry,*
> *and arduous enterprise.*

A visit to Dixmont offers a spacious view of the Dixmont Corner Cemetery as well as many historic buildings, such as the nearby Dixmont Corner Church. The church is a post–Federal period Gothic Revival Church that was built in 1834 and is considered one of the finest architectural examples of its kind in Maine.

WOODLAWN CEMETERY—ANDOVER

A true Maine treasure lies underneath a white marble gravestone at the Woodlawn Cemetery in Andover, Maine. To tell the story of Molly Ockett, a Native American woman of the Abenaki nation, in a few paragraphs really just offers highlights of a woman who bridged two very different and sometimes opposing worlds. It is estimated that she was born in 1740 in Saco, Maine, and that she spent much of her early life in the Fryeburg area. During King George's War (1744–48), she moved to Plymouth County, Massachusetts, where it is believed she learned to speak English. She then traveled back to Native American villages and settlements in Maine; however, the dangers of King Philip's War drove her to the St. Francis Mission in Quebec, Canada. Molly experienced the world she knew in Maine drastically changing during this time, as her people were killed and their land taken. It was also written that many Abenaki Indians were Catholic and received Christian names when they were baptized by French Catholic missionaries—one of the other names that Molly Ockett became known by was Mary Agatha.

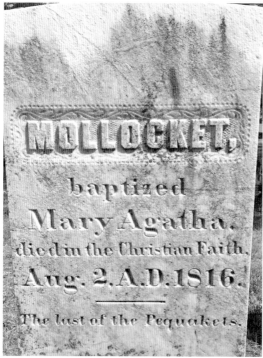

Above: The entrance to the Woodlawn Cemetery in Andover features a welcoming arched sign.

Left: The gravestone for "Molly Ockett" at the Woodlawn Cemetery in Andover.

Highly skilled in the uses of herbs, Molly was known for her ability to heal; she gained the respect of many of the white settlers. Molly even acted as a midwife and assisted in her friend Sarah Merrill's childbirth, which was the first child born in Andover, Maine, in July 1790. Some of the residents of Poland, Maine, alleged that Molly was a witch due to some intuitive predictions that she made, although they respected her healing abilities. During the winter of 1809, she tended to and cured a long illness that had nearly taken the life of the infant Hannibal Hamlin, who later became Abraham Lincoln's first vice president.

Molly was also quite the charismatic storyteller, and people just seemed to be drawn to all the tales of legends, lore and history that she shared. Some of those storytelling gatherings included Molly enjoying a half glass of rum, which many hosts accommodatingly poured for her. However, faith was also important to Molly, and there are accounts of her attending some particularly long church services in the Bethel area. Molly was known for speaking at Methodist meetings, something typically reserved only for men. Often Molly created and carried handicrafts, and a purse that she created out of twining porcupine quill, wool and hemp, woven with intricate geometric patterns, was donated to the Maine Historical Society in 1863.

The following account of Molly Ockett's last days is based on the reminiscences of Silvanus Poor of Andover and was recorded by his niece, Agnes Blake Poor, in her 1883 manuscript *Andover Memorials*:

> *In the spring of 1816, Mollockett* [sic] *being at the* [Richardson] *lakes, was taken ill at Beaver Brook, above the narrows on Lake Molechunkamunk. She was assisted down to Andover by some friendly Indians, who remained there about two weeks taking care of her. At the end of that time they represented to the authorities of the town that it would be better for the town to take charge of her, than to have the whole party on their hands, for if they stayed to take care of her they could not hunt and support themselves. They then left, and the town authorities took charge of her. They made a contract with Mr. Thomas Bragg to keep her the rest of her life. She so strongly objected to enter*[ing] *his house, saying, "Me want to die in a camp, that is the home for poor Indian," that a small camp was built for her, in which she remained till her death, receiving every attention necessary for her comfort. She was very patient in her last illness, and when asked if she were prepared to die, replied, "Me guess so, be here good many years." She died August 2, 1816, and was buried in the Andover graveyard. A funeral sermon was preached for her by the Rev. John Strickland, which*

was largely attended. A stone was erected to her memory, from the proceeds of a celebration held in Andover on the Fourth of July, 18[67] for that purpose. After her death, her effects, which were scattered about, some in Andover, some in Newry, etc., were collected and sold at public auction, and the proceeds were nearly sufficient to cover the expenses of her illness and burial. Some of these articles are still in existence, and I possessed at one time the pouch in which she was accustomed to carry her jewelry.

After Molly's death, there were many tales of hidden treasure she secretly stashed away. In a January 12, 1861 letter written to Dr. Nathaniel T. True of Bethel, Silvanus Poor of Andover, Maine, described the treasure legend. "The Last of the Pequakets: Mollocket" was published in the *Oxford Democrat* in 1863:

Tradition says that she formerly had quite a sum of money and that it was buried in a tea kettle on a small hill in the vicinity of White Cap [a high, granite-topped mountain in the northern part of Rumford], now called Farmer's Hill in this town, by the side of a large stone with a cross on it, and that there were guides to the large stone on smaller ones from a certain point in the Ellis River in the shape of an Indian arrow with barb and quiver. Much time was spent looking for it, but the trouble was to find the starting point. Several years ago, a Mr. F____ discovered the picture of an Indian's arrow on a stone in the woods. He stated the fact to an old gentleman who remembered the tradition. Search was immediately made, and the large stone marked with a cross was found. On digging about it they discovered that excavations had been made there before. It was Saturday and night came on before the money was found, and the secret leaked out. The party who had made the discovery went on Monday morning and reached the spot just in season to see two men depart with something like a kettle hanging upon a pole, and borne on their shoulders, who had been digging on the Sabbath and found the prize.

Molly Ockett's name lives on in other ways throughout the state of Maine. There is Molly Ockett's Cave in Fryeburg, Molls Rock on the eastern shore of Lake Umbagog and Moll Ockett Mountain in Woodstock.

KENNEBEC, MOOSE RIVER VALLEY, LAKES AND MOUNTAINS

Mount Vernon Cemetery, Augusta

Standing in the Mount Vernon Cemetery in Augusta, Maine, your eye might be attracted to the mausoleums or the many tilting marble gravestones along the tiers of the hillside. You will want to find your way down the hill to the far corner, near the tall, weathered maple tree at the edge of the cemetery. It is there that you will find a grave that tells a story from more than two hundred years ago that still strikes a chill memory in those who live in the city today.

The plaque on the stone reads:

> *Sacred to the Memory of Betsey Purrington, Mother, and her children: Polly, Benjamin, Anna, Nathaniel, Nathan, Louisa, and Margaret who were the victims of the Purrington tragedy. On July 9, 1806 they were murdered by their husband and father, Captain James Purrington, on their farm on the Old Belgrade Road. Also seriously wounded and survived was eldest son James. After a solemn funeral at the South Parish Church the victims were buried in an unmarked mass grave.*

> *This monument memorializes this sad episode in Augusta history and their recently discovered burial place. July 9, 2006.*

The 2006 memorial marker for the Purrington murder victims at the Mount Vernon Cemetery, Augusta.

The terrifying story starts in the hopeful marriage of Captain Purrington of Bowdoinham and Betsey Clifford from Bath. Betsey bore twelve children, four of whom died as infants. In 1805, the family moved to a farm in a quiet neighborhood on Old Belgrade Road in Augusta. The tragedy would take place just one year later. The questions regarding the reasoning behind these dark deeds were asked, but to this day they remain unanswered. Was it the fear of trying to maintain enough of the basic needs for a large family that drove Captain Purrington mad? Some accounts describe him as having what would be known today as bipolar disorder. Was there violence going on behind the closed doors of the farmhouse that we will never know?

The July 14, 1806 edition of the Portland, Maine *Gazette* recounted the story:

> *At an early hour on Wednesday morning last, the inhabitants of this town were alarmed with the dreadful information, that Capt. James Purinton, of this place, in cold blood, had murdered his wife, six children, and himself. His oldest son, with a slight wound, escaped, and his second daughter was found desperately wounded, and probably supposed dead by the father.*

Between the hours of 2 and 3 a near neighbour, Mr. Dean Wyman, was awakened by the lad who escaped, with an incoherent account of the horrid scene from which he had just fled; he, with a Mr. Ballard, another neighbour, instantly repaired to the fatal spot, and here, after having lighted a candle, a scene was presented which beggars all description.

In the outer room lay prostrate on his face, and weltering in his gore, the perpetrator of the dreadful deed—his throat cut in the most shocking manner, and the bloody razor lying on the table by his side. In an adjoining bed room lay Mrs. Purinton in her bed, her head almost severed from the body; and near her on the floor, a little daughter about ten years old, who probably hearing the cries of her mother, ran to her relief from the apartment in which she slept, and was murdered by her side.

In another apartment was found the two oldest and the youngest daughters, the first, aged 19, dreadfully butchered; the second desperately wounded, reclining with her head on the body of the dead infant 18 months old, and in a state of horror and almost total insensibility. In the room with the father, lay in bed with their throats cut, the two youngest sons, the one 8, the other 6 years old. And in another room was found on the hearth, most dreadfully mangled, the second son, aged 12; he had fallen with his trousers under one arm, with which he had attempted to escape.

On the breastwork over the fire-place was the distinct impression of a bloody hand, where the unhappy victim probably supported himself before he fell. The whole house seemed covered with blood, and near the body of the murdered laid the deadly axe. From the surviving daughter we have no account of this transaction; her dangerous situation prevents any communication, and but faint hopes are entertained for her recovery.

From the son, aged 17, we learn the following—That he was awaked by the piercing cries of his mother, and involuntarily shrieking himself, he leapt from his bed and ran towards the door of his apartment; he was met by his father with an axe in his hand (the moon shone bright) who struck him, but being so near each other, the axe passed over his shoulder and one corner of it entered his back, making a slight wound; his father then struck at him once or twice and missed him; at this moment his younger brother, who slept in the same bed with him, jumped from it, and attempted to get out at the door; to prevent this the father attacked him which gave the eldest an opportunity to escape. During this dreadful conflict, not a word was uttered.

From the appearance of the wounds generally, it seems to have been the design of Purinton to dissever the heads from the bodies, excepting the two youngest, whose throats it is supposed were cut with a razor. The oldest daughter and second son had several wounds, the probable consequence of their resistance. We have no evidence to lead us satisfactorily to the motives for this barbarous and unnatural deed.

Capt. Purinton was 46 years of age, and had lately removed from Bowdoinham to this town—an independent farmer, with a handsome estate, of steady, correct, and industrious habits, and of a good character and fair reputation, and strongly attached to his family. He had been heard lately to say, that he felt much distressed at the unpromising appearance of his farm; that he should be destitute of bread for his family, and hay for his cattle, and dreaded the consequences.

The Sunday before his death, it is said, he wrote to his brother and informed him that on the reception of the letter he should be dead, and requesting him to take charge of his family. In the letter was a death's head marked out, and it was sealed with black.—It was found on Monday by his wife, and gave her the greatest alarm and uneasiness. This her husband perceiving, and learning the cause, he attempted to console her by assurances that he had no intention of committing suicide, but that he had a presentiment of his approaching death.

Capt. Purinton was a warm believer in the doctrine of universal salvation, though it is not said of him, that he was a bigoted maniac or a religious enthusiast—his whole conduct the day preceding, and during the last and bloody scene of his life, seems marked with the utmost coolness and deliberation. Towards the close of that day he ground the fatal axe, and when the family retired to bed he was left reading the bible. The jury of inquest have brought him in guilty of wilful murder on his wife and six children, and that as a felon he did kill and murder himself—We do not recollect, that the annals of Massachusetts can furnish a transaction so distressing.

Further details on the story were discovered in *The History of Augusta*, published in 1870, which explained the scenes following the murder. The victims were each laid out in individual coffins at the local meetinghouse; Captain Purrington's remains were placed out on the porch with the murder weapons, the axe and the razor. By all descriptions, the attending crowd was immense, filling the streets and even assembled on rooftops. The mother and children were laid to rest in a grave that remained unmarked for two hundred years. Captain Purrington was buried with the murder weapons and without ceremony at the junction of Winthrop and Granite Streets.

The surviving Purrington son, James, according to records, moved out of state and had no descendants. Time passed, and in 2006, the Augusta Historic Preservation Commission decided to document the burial location of the family and placed a proper marker in honor of the victims and as a reminder of the tragedy of family violence.

Cony Cemetery, Augusta

Some people believe that to heal the past, you have to face uncomfortable and sometimes frightening realities, and the story of the unknown burials of more than eleven thousand people who were patients at the Augusta Mental Health Institute is a story that is being healed. It was first opened as the Maine Insane Hospital in Augusta, back in 1840. One could have never imagined the horrors that many of the patients would endure over the following 164 years. The patients were called "inmates," and some of the reasons why they were placed at the hospital seem unthinkable today. Suffering from epilepsy or sunstroke, having financial troubles or having disagreements with family members were some of the reasons for admission. While other people with much more severe issues were also part of the population, criminals and murderers were shipped there as well from jails and other facilities in the state. Some of those people with a violent past were known for taking their anger out on patients as well as staff, and there were several recorded murders that took place at the hospital. In 1868, Mary Peaslee had her face smashed into the floor by another inmate, over and over until she was dead. There were suicides, escapes and drownings in the nearby Kennebec River.

The grounds of the facility were beautiful, in contrast to some of the activities going on inside the building. There was a fountain and gardens, which attracted people to come and visit. However, the belief was also that the facility became a tourist attraction, with people coming to see the displays of the patients there. "Treatments" at the hospital included bleedings, shock treatment, opium and Thorazine therapies. There was even a "tranquilizer chair" that was used to restrain patients. By the 1950s, the facility had become overcrowded with roughly 1,800 inmates, far more than the 129 people it served when it opened. Around 1970, the name was changed to the Augusta Mental Health Institute (AMHI). Controversy and investigations into abuse continued over the next thirty years, until the facility was shut down in 2004.

First opened as the Maine Insane Hospital in Augusta in 1840, the building was closed in 2004 and now stands empty.

The work of the Cemetery Project Committee to honor the memory of the patients of the AHMI included the unveiling of this important memorial to their story.

In 2000, a Cemetery Project Committee was formed to look into the records of those who died at the AMHI. Initial reports yielded that only a few people died in the care of the facility. After deeper research, the number of people who died at AMHI was revealed to be 11,647 people, which was about a quarter of the total population that the facility served. A daily journal kept at the facility had an occasional note that mentioned when someone died at the hospital. There is also some speculation that some of the unclaimed patients may have been sent to Bowdoin College in the late 1800s and early 1900s and used for medical dissection. Where were the rest of the bodies buried? And why were there no records of what happened after their deaths? There was a handwritten map of the Cony Cemetery, which was across the street from AMHI; on the map, it indicated that there were at least 40 people from the hospital buried there, although most of them did not have proper gravestones.

Immediately, efforts were made to honor their memory with a memorial telling their story, finally unveiled in a ceremony on the hospital grounds. On that rainy day, most of the 11,647 names were read out loud and remembered. Afterward, the group walked over to see the memorial, which reads:

In Memory of the Patients who Died at the Augusta Mental Health Institute
AMHI

During the period of Augusta Mental Health Institute's operation, 1840– 2004, over 11,600 patients died while hospitalized there. Some were buried in their home communities. Some were buried in unmarked pauper's graves throughout Augusta. Some were buried in this cemetery a few in marked, most in unmarked graves. The location of the burial grounds for most of those patients who died at Augusta Mental Health Institute are unknown. Records were not kept or have been lost. May this stone serve as a memorial to those patients who died at AMHI. May it also serve as a reminder that their lives had value and that they were deserving of dignity both in life and in death.

BETHEL CEMETERIES AND BURIAL GROUNDS

One of the oldest villages in western Maine is Bethel, a community steeped in history and tradition and nestled among scenic vistas in the Oxford hills. If you want to explore the early recorded history of the area, the settlements and traditions of the Native Americans who lived here can be found in William Lapham's 1891 work, *History of Bethel, Maine*:

> *So common were the Indians during the first settlement of the town, that quite a fleet of canoes on the river was a common occurrence. On the banks of the Androscoggin, about one mile above the bridge* [that today carries U.S. Route 2 over the Androscoggin River], *and directly in front of the dwelling house of the late Timothy Chapman, Esq. there is an elevation of intervale consisting of three or four acres. It is a lovely spot wince about the year 1750. They had cleared about ten acres of the intervale for a corn field. Pine trees measuring eighteen inches in diameter had grown up in some places.*
>
> *On clearing the land, about twenty cellars were discovered, which had probably been used as a deposit for their corn. A dozen or more gun barrels were found, together with brass kettles, axes, knives, glass bottles, arrows and iron hoes, the latter of which were used by the settlers for several years afterwards, while the gun barrels were wrought into fire shovel handles by Fenmo, the blacksmith.*
>
> *A single skeleton was discovered wrapped in birch bark. It is said that they generally carried their dead to Canton Point for burial. Probably the settlement contained one or two hundred persons.*
>
> *A mile and a half below the bridge, near the Narrows, is Powow Point. Here they had a clearing of three-fourths of an acre, which seems to have been a place of rendezvous for hunters and warriors. There is a tradition that a camp was burned there with all its inmates, and that their implements and bones were afterwards found. Later the Indians made the point of land on Mill Brook their camping record.*

There are several cemeteries in Bethel, including the Riverside Cemetery just off Route 2, which started as a family cemetery and was once known as the Mayville Cemetery. Gravestones at the cemetery date back to the late 1700s. The cemetery is still being used today by the community.

Located along Route 5 in Bethel is the Woodland Cemetery. This site is the final resting place for two congressmen and a host of other notable

The entrance to the Woodland Cemetery in Bethel, Maine, features a variety of terraces for many burials.

people. In this cemetery, you will find a gravestone that reads, "Ernest Martin Skinner, Great American Organ Builder." Ernest died at the age of ninety-four on November 25, 1960. He was an innovator in his field. For a time, he actually spent more on building his famous pipe organs than he sold each of them for. His attention to detail garnered him a strong following and steady customers. One of the best examples of his pipe organs can be found in Woolsley Hall at Yale University.

Another grave that has an interesting epitaph is that of Brigadier General Clark Swett Edwards; carved on his stone is the quote, "I will not ask for a leave of absence while within the heaving of the booming of Rebel cannon." General Edwards participated in nearly every major battle during the Civil War, including among them First and Second Bull Runs, Fredericksburg, Gettysburg and Spotsylvania. By July 1864, as the colonel in command of the Fifth Regiment, he was notable for capturing six Confederate flags and taking more than 1,200 prisoners and 1,700 small arms. For gallantry in action, he was brevetted brigadier general of U.S. volunteers on March 13, 1865.

The gravestone for Brigadier General Clark S. Edwards features crossed swords and one of his famous quotes.

General Edwards was well respected, and when the war was over, he refused to return to their slaveholders those who were enslaved and had escaped across enemy lines. He was also known for taking as many precautions as he could to spare the lives of those in his command and often stood at a distance in front of his troops, standing in the direct lines of cannon fire. After the war, he returned home and pursued his interests in agriculture and business.

General Edwards married only once and had two children, and he died at the age of seventy-nine on May 3, 1903. An excerpt from his obituary reads:

> *He gave up the battle of life on the anniversary of his fight at Salem Church forty years ago. At the outbreak of the war he was a contractor and builder, but dropped his tools upon the work on which he was engaged when the news came to him of the firing on Fort Sumter, and telegraphed the governor for authority to raise a company.*

He was remembered in newspapers throughout the United States as a "Gallant Veteran," and today his remains lie under a carved pair of crossed swords on a gravestone in Bethel, Maine.

UNEARTHING THE GHOSTS

The Walking Ghost—Dixmont, Maine

In the early 1900s, there was the story of the "walking ghost" in Dixmont. According to the tale, "Just the expression on the face of a person who happens to be telling of an experience in that house at night, is enough to convince the most rabid unbeliever." The incident causing the mysterious happenings was said to have occurred in the 1860s. A traveling salesman had been passing through the town and was looking for lodging one night. A local man opened the doors of his home to the traveler and offered to board him for the night. The man was described as "unscrupulous" when it came to financial dealings.

Townsfolk never saw the man leave the house the next morning—in fact, he was never seen again. Whispers and rumors began that the bones of the peddler were buried in a brick vault in the basement of the house he was last seen entering. The owner of the house allegedly built this stone recess to cover up the dark deed that he had committed. For further proof of the claim about the grave in the basement, the story continued that one day the owner's dog was digging and tearing up the ground around the area as the owner was installing a wooden sill. As people gathered along the road to speculate, the owner became a "wild man," sweating profusely and looking quite nervous. He ran and grabbed his gun and shot his own dog for fear that his secret would be revealed.

Just before the death of this man's wife, she wrote to her sister who lived hundreds of miles away to tell her that there was something that she needed to confide in her. Strangely, two months after the woman's death, her sister came to town and married her husband, never knowing what she had wanted to tell her.

It was also rumored that there were two possible witnesses to the murder and that they died quickly and mysteriously. Bertram L. Smith, who was the county attorney from Patten, was investigating one of those deaths. The man had been shot and killed on his front doorstep by an unknown assailant. The other witness was found in another state, drowned in a pond. Neither case was ever solved.

The walking ghost in Dixmont was described as being seen in the "dead hours" of the night, creeping up and down the stairs of the house, followed by the sound of a moaning whimper. The echoes of a person walking down the stairs, dragging something heavy with them, are then heard. Some believers in the ghost claimed that they heard in the house the sound of blood dripping onto the chamber floor.

The whole story made headlines in the June 5, 1905 edition of the *Bangor Daily News*: "Obliging Ghost Comes to Be Murdered Every Night." A grainy black-and-white photo accompanies the story of two dwellings at the top of a hill; the caption reads, "Here is where the ghost walks." Are there still some old, moldering bones buried in an old brick vault, yet to be discovered, in Dixmont? And even more curious the question: does the ghost still walk there?

GLIDDEN CEMETERY, NEWCASTLE

Some ghost stories leave the listeners with so many questions that they might be prompted to go and look into it themselves. The riverside Glidden Cemetery in Newcastle, Maine, is just the perfect place to wander under tall trees and over burial mounds in the search for answers to one particular question: Was Mary Howe buried alive?

The Howe family has roots in early New England as some of the first settlers to arrive to the New World. Eventually, in the nineteenth century, the family migrated up into Darmiscotta, Maine, leaving behind many stories of hard work and success along the way. Mary Howe was a Spiritualist and practiced séances at a popular tavern that became known as the Plummer's

Do the mysteries of the Glidden Cemetery in Newcastle manifest as a wandering spirit?

House. From all accounts, the show that Mary put on was really something to see, and people traveled from miles around. Mary had become such a strong believer in her faith that, on one occasion, she even thought she could fly. She climbed to the top of the staircase and took a swan dive into the air, even though her "flying" consisted of her sustaining a broken ankle and some bumps when she landed at the bottom.

There was some skepticism about Mary's abilities by some; however, many people became believers after one particular prediction that she made. Mary had a vision of the relative of a guest who attended one of her séances—the relative was away in New York at the time. Incredibly, she described that she saw him surrounded by many lights, and she said that the moment the lights appeared he was going to die. A few days later, word arrived that the man she saw in the vision died at the exact same time the lights were turned on at the Brooklyn Bridge.

Mary would often go into trances, where she would become unconscious and seem barely alive. In the summer of 1882, Mary went in a deep trance—reportedly for an entire week! Mary's brother, Edwin, who assisted in the public séances, often placed stones around her body to help her retain body heat during the experience. People lined up at the house to see the spectacle, and another week passed with her not having awoken from the trance. Dr. Dixon was summoned, and he examined Mary and pronounced her dead, even though her face was still warm and there were no signs of rigor mortis. Newspaper reporters visited and reported the sensational story, and everyone wanted to get a look at Mary. Finally, there was a debate as whether to bury Mary or not—what if they were burying her alive? An undertaker was summoned by the doctor and the authorities, although Edwin strongly protested.

It wasn't an easy task to find an undertaker willing to bury Mary. Eventually, an undertaker took on the job, but even his assistant was hesitant. The ground was opened, the body of Mary Howe was covered with earth and the grave was filled. For days and weeks after, people in the community were afraid of passing by the cemetery for fear of what or who they might see. Rumors followed for years about the cemetery being haunted by strange noises and odd-looking lights. Was Mary buried alive, suffocated by the grave dirt—or was she really dead? To this day, no one has been able to answer the question.

DEAD MAN'S GULCH, WALES, MAINE

One of the biggest claims to fame for Leeds Junction, Maine, is its important role in the railroad history of Maine. Officially now part of Wales, Maine, Leeds Junction was an important rail center connecting major lines like Portland and Brunswick with more remote parts of the state. While it was first called Leeds Crossing because the two lines intersected there, later the lines became part of the Maine Central Railroad. Wales took its name in the eighteenth century from some of the settlers who came over from that country in the United Kingdom. Wales has seen some growth in recent memory with the addition of several Amish families who have moved to farms in the town.

An area called Dead Man's Gulch was once part of Leeds Junction, described as a wild and lonely spot near an old logging road. The stories from there are bone-chilling. In the early 1900s, a local man was struck by a train that was traveling through the Gulch. The body of a wandering vagrant was also found in the exact area some months before, and that's how the location came to be named.

On a Sunday morning in November 1904, the body of Augustus Hoffman was found hanging from the limb of a tree at Dead Man's Gulch. Two men who were passing through the area discovered the body along the steep bank about seven rods from the railroad track. Several short pieces of rope had been pieced together, and a sailor's noose was crafted; one end was fastened to a small tree about four feet from the ground. Upon a closer examination, it was determined that the man placed his head through the noose, leaned back and met his demise. The man had been well dressed, wearing a suit and a tidy black overcoat along with a black cap. In his pockets was a bill that was dated November 4, 1904, for three weeks' room and board at the Sanborn and Rowe boardinghouse in Bridgton. There was also a diary in his pocket with the word *Lewiston* written over the month of November. He had less than one dollar on him, and he wore a Waltham watch that had stopped at 3:30.

The coroner traveled from Augusta and determined that it was a suicide, as there was no evidence of struggle or foul play. W.L. Churchill, a local storekeeper, said that he thought he recognized the man as having stopped by a few days earlier; a bag found in the man's pocket confirmed that he had made a purchase from the store. News traveled from Bridgton that the man had been working in the woolen mill there for three weeks, filling in, and that he had left about a week earlier. He had been seen on his way to Lewiston, drinking heavily, after leaving Bridgton, with a roll of money on his person. It was later discovered that his wife had passed away previously, and he had two young children living in Manchester, Maine. For a time after the discovery the locals talked about Dead Man's Gulch being haunted.

MILLINOCKET CEMETERY, MILLINOCKET

The town of Millinocket saw a boom of growth in 1900 due to the establishment of the Great Northern Paper Company in the previous year. The need for a paper mill was driven by the popularity and consumption of newspapers, which began to explode in the nineteenth century. Immigrants moved into the town, having traveled from all over Europe. In 1902, the residents of Millinocket were dealing with an outbreak of smallpox and diphtheria. In 1903, typhoid cases were multiplying at an alarming rate, overburdening the community with temporary needs for housing those who were ill. The boardinghouse in town had become overwhelmed, so the town purchased a small house, known as a "pest house," to quarantine those who were stricken with the illness. Shortly afterward, a second "pest house" was built that had two floors; it also filled quickly.

Around this challenging time for the town, the Millinocket Cemetery was established, and it is still being used today for interments. Along one of the pathways is a white marble marker with a faint letter *L* carved into it. The text on the first line of the stone reads, "William Lahey, April 19, 1855–December 14, 1906." William was a laborer who was accidentally mistaken for a deer and shot and killed by Charles Pillsbury of Hartland, Maine. Mr. Pillsbury turned himself into authorities, and he was held on the charge of manslaughter.

William Lahey's wife moved out of the house on Central Street in Millinocket. Sometime after she moved out, a woman named Mrs. Allen, who also lived in the house, complained that there were strange noises coming from the apartment that the family had occupied. She claimed to have heard a sewing machine operating in the apartment, along with other disturbing noises. She described hearing wood logs and trunks being loudly moved around the room. Mrs. Allen said that one evening, she heard footsteps as if someone were walking around in the space. She lit a lamp and went and explored the empty rooms, but she found nothing and no one there.

Word quickly spread throughout town about the alleged hauntings happening in William Lahey's former apartment, and it remained unoccupied. A respected female resident of the town was so intrigued that she went to explore the apartment to decide for herself. The woman spent a considerable amount of time investigating the location, and she confirmed the stories that Mrs. Allen told.

The editor of the *Millinocket Journal* newspaper, R.A. Brown, decided to make several visits to the location seeking evidence of the ghostly inhabitants. Then three members of the board of selectmen decided that they wanted to investigate too. The owner of the building, Mr. Tapley, got tired of the constant interruptions and had the three men arrested for trespassing. They settled out of court and paid a fine of $50. Finally, in April 1907, three more residents of the town wanted to look into the ghost story as well. These men let their curiosity get to them, and they were also arrested for trespassing. They each paid their $200 bail money and appeared in the Millinocket Superior Court, where the case was continued and amicably settled.

All remains quiet today at the grave of William Lahey. He sleeps beneath the stone with his wife, Ellen, who passed in 1920, and their son, Chester, who passed just shy of the age of two in 1901.

CRESCENT BEACH CEMETERY, CAPE ELIZABETH

Located in a small burial ground next to the Inn by the Sea in Cape Elizabeth, Maine, is a gravestone that recounts a very dramatic story:

> *Sacred to the memory of*
> *MISS LYDIA CARTER*
> *daut'r of Mr Amos Carter of Freeport*
> *AE 21 who with 15 other unfortunate*
> *passengers male and female perished*
> *in the merciless waves by the shipwreck*
> *of the schooner Charles Capt. Jacob Adams*
> *bound from Boston to Portland*
> *on a reef of rocks near the shore of*
> *Richmond's Island on Sunday night*
> *July 12, 1807*

This tragically romantic tale is the story of the "ghost bride" of Cape Elizabeth, Lydia Carver. Lydia was one of seven children of Amos Carver, who had become a wealthy Portland businessman. Her family had moved to nearby Freeport from the Plymouth area of Massachusetts. Unfortunately, there are not many personal details known about Lydia herself or about the man she was supposed to marry. But what is certain is that her sad tale began in July 1807.

An excited twenty-three-year-old Lydia, along with twenty-one other people (mostly her bridal party), boarded the schooner *Charles* and set out to Boston, Massachusetts, to have her wedding gown fitted. The captain of the ship was Jacob Adams of Portland, who had brought along his wife.

On Sunday, July 12, the schooner sailed off from Boston to complete the overnight trip back to Portland. It was said to be a bright and sunny summer day as the *Charles* made good time on the return journey. As the schooner approached Richmond's Island, just before midnight, a severe gale seemed to blow in out of nowhere, and tragedy seemed imminent. The Atlantic Ocean roared, and towering waves overcame the *Charles*. The swells caused the schooner to strike Watt's Ledge, just fifty feet offshore from Richmond's Island. The schooner tipped over onto its side, and the bottom of the *Charles* was ripped out.

The passengers on the *Charles* faced their doom in the cold ocean waters as the waves washed over the wrecked schooner. Some of the passengers attempted to cling to the ship's rigging; however, they were no match for the stormy sea. Captain Adams and three other men attempted to reach the shore of Richmond's Island. Frantic cries from Adams's wife called him back to the ship, and as he attempted to return to her, the waves carried him off to a watery grave.

Those who tried to find a way to hold on to the remains of the schooner were forced into the sea as the *Charles* broke apart during the late night hours. When the storm passed and the morning sun appeared, a devastating scene revealed itself on nearby Crescent Beach. The body of Lydia Carver had washed ashore, and next to her was her trunk, holding her never-to-be-worn bridal gown. In all, sixteen people perished that fateful July night. The bodies of the captain and his wife were also recovered, and they were buried at the Eastern Cemetery in Portland. Lydia's body was buried at a little countryside burial ground just above Crescent Beach.

There are about twenty gravestones in the burial ground, some newer than the stone for Lydia. It is Lydia's stone that seems to be in the best condition, as it is totally readable. I learned about Lydia's story when I received a call some years back from the nearby Inn by the Sea, which originally opened in 1982. There were a surprising number of ghost stories coming from the inn regarding sightings of Lydia wearing her white wedding gown. I made several visits to the Inn over the following years and, in fact, even had a large dinner gathering there. During that gathering, I met an older woman from the Cape Elizabeth Historical Society who had quite a ghost story to share. She told me that in the 1960s, her daughter caught a glimpse of Lydia on nearby Route 77. There are lush meadows and small forested areas along this very scenic but typically quiet road that leads past the inn. I was told that as the young woman was traveling in her car, she noticed two figures standing by the side of the road. As the woman approached, she discovered a lady wearing a long, white wedding gown standing silently, resting her hand on a female deer that stood completely still at her side. The woman in the gown made eye contact with the traveler on Route 77, and then as the car passed, she vanished; a look in the rearview mirror revealed that there was no one there. The woman's daughter was absolutely certain that she had seen the ghost of Lydia Carver that night.

The people who worked at the Inn by the Sea believed that Lydia would appear from time to time in the mirrors in the hotel and that she took an occasional ride on their elevator. There is a portrait of Lydia Carver that hangs in the inn, and oddly enough, no one knows where it came from or how it got there—it was just always there. There were tales from the restaurant about place settings and dishes being moved around without explanation. Staff also believed that the spirit of Lydia might be taking care of her gravestone, which might explain why it's always in such spotless shape. In recent years, there have been fewer reports of Lydia sightings at the inn, as it has become quite a popular wedding destination. However, there are still stories and sightings of her walking on nearby Crescent Beach.

THE EASTERN CEMETERY, PORTLAND

One of the oldest burial grounds in Maine, the Eastern Cemetery was officially established in 1668; however, it is said that interments began earlier than that. George Cleeve, one of the original settlers, who is often referred to as the father of Portland, designated this land to be used as a burial ground. When he passed away in 1666, he was buried just behind his home, which was customary at the time. Soon thereafter, the cemetery around him was officially established. Unfortunately, it is said that Cleeve's remains were uprooted just two hundred years later, after Portland's Great Fire of 1866.

A view through the gates of the Eastern Cemetery in Portland.

As the reconstruction of local sites began, a retaining wall was built along Federal Street. In doing so, part of the hillside and burial ground was dug out, along with Cleeve's remains. The earth (and what resided in it) was used for construction fill.

In the nineteenth century, this six-acre burial ground was referred to as the "field of ancient graves." Originally surrounded by a mossy stone wall, the cemetery once boasted an enormous tall Norway pine tree that was so large it could be seen in the distance by those entering Portland Harbor. Some of the first people buried here were the victims of Native American raids, including the twelve men who were killed on September 21, 1689, near the Deering mansion, as well as another thirteen men who were killed by a party of Native Americans in an ambush close to the cemetery just a few years later.

In the cemetery you will find the memorial to Colonel William Tyng, who received his commission from British general Gage in Boston in 1774. He later fled to New York and Nova Scotia but returned to Maine in 1793 and settled in nearby Gorham, where he passed away in 1807. This ten-foot-high monument of red freestone and marble panels was commissioned by his wife. There is also the grave of Daniel Manly, who holds the distinction of being Portland's first bank robber in 1818. Two men, Thomas Bird and Solomon Goodwin, are also buried here; they were hanged for murder in the late eighteenth century.

There are about seventy-five underground tombs in the cemetery as well, although it has been said that they have collapsed over the years from the shifting of the ground caused by burials and visitors. According to cemetery records, the cemetery is the final resting place for more than four thousand of the city's earliest residents. Space for burials became quite cramped, so many remains were buried inordinately close to one another and at unusual angles, according to records.

A plaque stands just outside the cemetery that informs visitors that the burial ground is the final resting place for many abolitionists. People who provided safe houses as part of the Underground Railroad, campaigned against slavery and assisted African Americans to freedom are remembered here.

Many of those buried here are easily linked to the sea with a review of the epitaphs. One stone reads, "Lost at Sea," while another reads, "Executed for murder on the high seas." Still another reads, "Killed by a fall from a masthead." There are also numerous unmarked graves throughout the cemetery. Located in the southwest corner of the grounds was an area for Quaker burials. There are also two unmarked sections that served as Black burial grounds. Another section, called the "Strangers" section, was set aside for the poor and unknown; this section is also unmarked. Oddly enough, the City of Portland allowed for the burial of two bodies per grave in the "Strangers" area.

Near the Congress Street entrance stands a small Gothic Revival cottage, under which was the city tomb, which was used during the winter months. It was reported that in 1868 there were 111 bodies awaiting burial in the spring, when the ground thawed. Today, this attractive building is used as a storage shed for the cemetery. Interments ended in 1858, when the cemetery was filled to capacity. Just next door to the cemetery is the North School, which was renovated in the 1980s as senior housing.

Also, along the Congress Street entrance is a beautiful black iron fence and gate, which were salvaged some years ago from renovations at the Portland High School. The fence adds to the Gothic charm of the entrance to the burial ground. It is said that while peering through the fence, you might see some of the ancient ghostly spirits of the Eastern Cemetery. According to local legend, a midnight discussion is carried on in the burial ground by two sworn and bitter enemies. The spirits are said to be those of Captain Samuel Blyth, commander of the British warship *Boxer*, and Lieutenant William Burrows, commander of the American ship *Enterprise* during the War of 1812. The intense battle took place just north of Casco Bay, off Monhegan Island, and sadly resulted in the deaths of both men. The *Enterprise* was victorious and brought the captured British ship into Portland. Side by side, the two men were buried in the Eastern Cemetery, both with full military honors.

Their apparitions are said to appear by their grave sides, engaged in a loud shouting match, perhaps still engaged in a war of words. Those who have witnessed the confrontation claim that as soon as the spirits notice they are being watched by someone, they disappear behind the gravestones, leaving no trace except for a fine mist. Perhaps coincidentally, a nonprofit volunteer organization called Spirits Alive works for the preservation and protection of the cemetery through public events, workshops and tours.

SPEAKING STONES

Epitaphs to Remember

The mysterious moment of death proves to be a moment of waking.
How one longs to take it for one's self!
—Sarah Orne Jewett

Epitaph is a noun that comes to us from Medieval Latin in the fourteenth century. It is an inscription on or at a tomb or grave in memory of the one buried there. It can also be a brief statement commemorating or epitomizing a deceased person or something past.

OLD YORK BURIAL GROUND, YORK, MAINE

Here are deposited the Remains
of Elizabeth Wood
The Curtain of Death Conceald her
from mortal view
on the 7th day of May AD 1801
in the 23rd year of her age
We believe (if the reward of virtue is HEAVEN)
She will shine in immortal youth
She will act
Without other ornaments; than Heavens own Scenery
On a theatre who maker and builder is GOD

A distant view of the Stevens Cemetery in Sweden.

STEVENS CEMETERY, TAPAWINGO ROAD, SWEDEN, MAINE

> *Mr. Jacob Stevens*
> *Died Jan. 22, 1831:*
> *AE 75 y'rs, 5 mos. 14 days*
> *He was the first settler in Sweden*

Tapawingo is an American Indian word that means "house of happiness."

VILLAGE CEMETERY, FRYEBURG, MAINE

> *Sarah Griswold*
> *Wife of Oliver Griswold*
> *died July 7, 1836*
> *Et. 60*
> *Daughter of Rev. William Fessenden*
> *A friend to the friendless*
> *A mother to the orphan*

Someone still puts flowers on the grave for Sarah Griswold at the Village Cemetery in Fryeburg.

HARRINGTON MEETINGHOUSE CEMETERY, PEMAQUID, MAINE

In memory of Mrs. Mathew Fossett
Consort of Mr. Alexr. Fossett
Who departed this life on Octr 26th, 1802.
Aged 31 years & 11 months
She was the mother of eight children
seven of which with her husband stood
Around her while she bore the pains of
death with great fortitude and mildness.

Also Mr. Alex Fossett Junr.
Son of Mr. Alexr & Mrs. Mathew Fossett
Who departed this life
(in the borough of Norfolk in Virginia)
Janry 1st, 1800 Aged 18 years, 10 mo & 10 days
His body was interred in the old Church yard in Norfolk.

Why do we mourn departed friends
Or shake at death's alarms
Tis but the voice that Jesus sends
To call them to his arms.

VILLAGE CEMETERY, KENNEBUNKPORT, MAINE

Capt. Leander Foss AE 36.
was lost in the wreck of the new
Barque Isidore together with all
on board, 15 in number on Cape
Neddick Nov. 30, 1842
May this event God sanctify
And thus prepare us all to die
That when we leave this earthly clod,
We may be bless'd and dwell with GOD.

The ship the *Isidore* wrecked on the Bald Head cliffs in Cape Neddick as it was making its way back to port during a severe storm. Since the 1880s, there have been stories published about the phantom ship sailing the southern coast of Maine.

STIMSON FAMILY BURIAL PLOT, KITTERY, MAINE

> *David S.*
> *son of*
> *Charles & Eliza*
> *STIMSON*
> *Accidentally killed at the*
> *Kittery Navy Yard*
> *Nov. 13, 1842*
> *Aged 19 yrs 9 mos 13 d's*

VARNEY CEMETERY, BRUNSWICK, MAINE

> *Sacred to the memory of*
> *George Cobb*
> *Born June 10, 1794*
> *Died Nov. 10, 1843*
> *AEt. 88 yrs*
> *Fell asleep on May 9, 1882*

George's gravestone indicates his spiritual "rebirth" when he converted to Christianity and was baptized on November 10, 1843; he lived for nearly forty years afterward.

CONCLUSION

I find it very difficult to write the conclusion to this book, because honestly I don't want to stop sharing stories of Maine's graveyards. But alas, there is only so much room between these pages. In putting this book together, I wanted to tell the stories of some people individually, while other chapters spoke of cemeteries as a whole. The goal was to tell stories of the people who are part of the fabric of Maine—both the famous, buried in grand tombs, and those not so famous, hidden away in elusive family burial grounds.

There is so much more ground to cover in Maine, and there are so many stones and stories I've still yet to discover. The stories in this book were collected from countless graveyard explorations over the years and time spent digging through archival materials. Often when you find me planning a trip throughout the state, I'll search out the locations of the cemeteries before I even make hotel reservations. After the trips, I'll spend weeks putting the materials together for presentations and possible future tours. I currently have about fifteen thousand photos of gravestones stored in the virtual cloud.

I also wanted to make a brief note on preservation of graveyards—without them, so much history and so many stories are lost. It is evident that much has been done in recent years to restore many gravestones and cemeteries in Maine, and that work must continue, as each year the stones deteriorate a little more and the stories of the people beneath them grow

Left: A memorial stained-glass window with an anchor motif at St. Ann's Episcopal Church in Kennebunkport.

Below: A receiving tomb in Oakland. These tombs were used to store the bodies of people who died during the winter, when the ground was too frozen to dig graves.

ever distant. Seek out organizations in your community or nonprofit groups that are working on cemetery restoration or documentation projects.

My hope is that you will find this book a handy guide for your own cemetery travels and explorations. There are more legendary stories to be discovered and gravestones to be read out there. Who will you meet, and what will their stones tell you?

AUTHOR'S NOTES

Always be respectful and cautious when you tread on these museums of stone, as the smallest remnant of an old gravestone could be underneath your feet, likely from a winter frost heave or the steady shifting of the grounds. Gravestone rubbings are prohibited in Maine, but here's a better suggestion: if you are looking to read the inscriptions on the stones, carry a mirror with you to shine light onto the carvings.

Here are some field exercises:

- Find the gravestone of someone who was in the military. How can you tell that he/she was in the military? What was his/her name and date of death? Can you determine which war this person died in or served in by the dates on his/her tombstone?

- Find a tombstone of a child. How do you know it is that of a child? How old was the child? Can you tell how he/she died? What does the artwork or the tombstone design tell you about the child or the parents of the child? Were they wealthy or poor? How can you tell?

- What is the oldest tombstone that you located? Describe what you know about the person by his/her tombstone.

- Record the details of the most interesting tombstone (design or epitaph) that you have found.

- Can you tell anything about the community or the neighborhood by investigating the tombstones of those who were buried in this cemetery?

- Can you tell if the gravestone is signed? Does it have any symbols or designs near the bottom?

BIBLIOGRAPHY

Bangor Daily News. "Complains About Too Many Dry Bones." July 23, 1912, 10.

————. "Death Thursday of Sarah Orne Jewett." June 25, 1909, 1.

————. "Exhumed Several Bodies While Excavating for Cellar on Union Street." September 12, 1908, 8.

————. "Gray Remembers Unknown Soldier, a Confederate Sent North by Error." May 30, 1977, 15.

————. "Monument to Those Forcibly Removed from Coastal Island Dedicated at Pineland Farms." July 15, 2017.

————. "Opening of Camden Turnpike Recalls Early Tragedy." July 23, 1915, 14.

————. "Plaque Proposed at Poor House Cemetery." May 4, 1994, 19.

————. "Sad Tales Remember Young Women's Deaths." June 12, 1981, 15.

Blanchard, Paula. *Sarah Orne Jewett: Her World and Her Work.* Boston: Da Capo Press, 1994.

Boston Gazette and Country Journal. Notices, February 18, 1771.

Boston Globe. "Fortune Hers, as Death Came." July 19, 1911, 8.

Boston Post. "Disasters." March 25, 1876, 4.

Bouchard, Kelley. "Maine's Forgotten Dead." *Portland Press Herald,* May 27, 2012.

Brown, Leonard. *American Patriotism: Or, Memoirs of "Commen Men."* Des Moines, IA: Redhead and Wellslager, 1869.

Crosby, Craig. "New AMHI Memorial Unveiled in Augusta." *Kennebec Journal*, September 18, 2015.

Dorr, Zac. "AMHI Memorial." *Times Record*, September 9, 2018.

Drake, Samuel Adams. *New England Legends and Folklore in Prose and Poetry*. New York: Little, Brown and Company Publishers, 1910.

Federal Writers' Project. "Maine: A Guide Down East." Book Collections at the Maine State Library, 1937. https://digitalmaine.com/books/59.

First Annual Report of the State Board of Charities and Corrections, 1913. Waterville, ME: Sentinel Publishing Company.

Goold, William. *Portland in the Past: With Historical Notes of Old Falmouth*. Portland, ME: Heritage Books Inc., 1997.

Inland Fisheries and Wildlife Documents. "Report of the Commissioners of Inland Fisheries and Game, 1906" (1907): 194.

Lapham, William B. "History of Bethel, Formerly Sudbury, Canada, Oxford County, Maine 1768–1890 with a Brief Sketch of Hanover and Family Statistics." *Maine Town Documents* (1891): 783. https://digitalcommons.library.umaine.edu/towndocs/783.

MacPherson, Rick. "Tales from the Boneyard." *Casco Bay Weekly*, October 26, 1995.

Maine Historical Society. *Collections of the Maine Historical Society* 2 (1847).

Marble, A.P. *The New England Magazine and Bay State Monthly* (1887). Published by J.N. McClintock, Kennebec County, Maine.

Mount Hope Cemetery Virtual Tour. "Amanda Skofield Memorial." https://mounthopecemetery.omeka.net/items/show/17.

New York Times. "Reminiscence of the Lost Steamship Pacific." August 7, 1861, 5.

Pickett, Darla L. "History Lives for Embden Woman." *Bangor Daily News*, June 14, 1983, 14.

Poor, Agnes Blake. *Andover Memorials*. 2nd ed. Bryant Pond, ME: Inman Publishing, 1997. Originally published in 1883.

Porter, John W., ed. *Maine Historical Magazine* 9 (January 1894–January 1895).

Portland Press Herald. "Reminders of Early Cat Mousam, Farm Burying Ground." September 19, 1948, 68.

Portsmouth Herald. "Kittery Point First Congregational Church Won Hard Battle for Survival." August 6, 1964, 2.

Schreiber, Laurie. *Tall Barney: A Beals Island Legend Lives On*. Rockland, ME: Island Institute Publishing, June 18, 2014.

Seymour, Tom. "History of Belfast." *Fisherman's Voice* 17, no. 12 (December 2012).

Skinner, Charles Montgomery. *Myths and Legends of Our Own Land*. Philadelphia, PA: J.P. Lippincott Company Publishers, 1896.

Thornton, Nellie C. *Traditions and Records of Southwest Harbor and Somesville*. Bar Harbor, ME: Acadia Publishing, 1988. Originally published in 1938.

Warren, George Augustus, MD, and Henry Warren Wheeler. *The History of Brunswick, Topsham, and Harpswell: Including the Ancient Territory Known as Pejepscot*. Boston: A Mudge & Sons, Printers, 1878. https://digitalcommons.library.umaine.edu/towndocs/783.

Welch, T.B. "Dental Literature." *The Dental Independent* 12 (1890). Philadelphia, Pennsylvania.

York County Coast Star. "Cemeteries Squeezed." March 21, 2002.

MAINE OLD CEMETERY ASSOCIATION

The Maine Old Cemetery Association was founded in 1968 to foster interest in the discovery, restoration and maintenance of Maine cemeteries, as well as to preserve records and historical information that relate to them. https://www.moca-me.org.

ABOUT THE AUTHOR

Dubbed "Maine's Mystery Maven" by the *York County Coast Star*, Roxie Zwicker has been entertaining the locals, visitors from away and curious souls with her unique storytelling abilities since 1994. Her company, New England Curiosities, located in Portsmouth, New Hampshire, has been offering lectures, tours, spooky trolley rides and special haunted events since 2002 and is consistently on top of the nation's travel and tourism lists. Featured on *Psychic History* on the History Channel and *Destination America* on the Travel Channel, Roxie is the author of eight books on New England's history, ghost stories and folklore. In addition to running a successful ghost tour company, Roxie travels throughout the Northeast, doing countless speaking engagements on haunted history as well as acting as a consultant for haunted attractions. She is the hostess of the podcast *Wicked Curious Radio*, which can be found on iTunes, Buzzsprout and Soundcloud. Her website is www.newenglandcuriosities.com, and her Instagram is RoxieZw.

Visit us at
www.historypress.com